FALLING OFF A HORSE

IN THE FALKLAND ISLANDS

by

E Colgate

I hope you enjoy the book.
Edward

George Mann Publications

Published by
George Mann Publications
Easton, Winchester
Hampshire SO21 1ES
01962 779944

A CIP record for this publication
is available from the British Library

ISBN 0954163427

George Mann Publications

Falling Off a Horse in the Falkland Islands.

Discover the Old Falklands Islands Life - Compare the New.

Here is an entertaining book about daily life in the Falkland Islands as encountered by a travelling teacher living with families on the sheep farms.
1962- Sheep littered islands isolated in the windswept South Atlantic should not have much to offer but the Falkland Islands prove otherwise.
PEOPLE GREAT   SCENERY WILD   WEATHER ANNOYING
1982- Determination. Letters from families caught in the 'conflict'.
2002- Time has moved on. The islands in the 21st century.

FALLING OFF A HORSE IN THE FALKLAND ISLANDS.
E.COLGATE.

160 pages, fully illustrated colour and B & W. Map, glossary, index.
SBN 0954163427   Published by GEORGE MANN PUBLICATIONS
Available through some bookshops but quicker direct from
E. Colgate, 7 South View Terrace, HENFIELD, West Sussex, BN5 9ES.
PRICE £10. UK p&p free: overseas £2 a book; cheque /P.O to E.Colgate.

CONTENTS

ILLUSTRATIONS

**To Robin and the memory of Peggy who gave me the little
newspaper advertisement that led to the Falkland Islands.
And to Falkland Islands friends remembered here.**

ACKNOWLEDGEMENTS

Thank you, all of you who have kindly agreed to being in the book and thank you, Clara, Margie and Tony, for the use of the letters in the last chapter.

Thanks, Frances, for being an extremely understanding wife. Thanks, children; Bob, for organising the purchase of the computer for me; Andrew, Heather, Jenny and husband Jon, for teaching me sufficient of its mannerisms to enable me to cope. Thank you, Maureen, for recommending a publishing team. Thanks, family at large, for putting up with me going on about 'my book' ad infinitum.

Thank you, Barbara Large, for your calm and encouraging editorship. Thank you, George Mann, for your patient guidance through to the published end product.

Thank you, Suky Cameron, for your interest and help at the Falkland Islands Office in London. It was wonderful being there among reminders of the islands and being received so hospitably.

A great big thank you to Leona Whitney for that fantastic evening you gave Frances and me when we visited you asking cheeky questions during your brief visit to U.K. Thanks too, to Vi Masters for making it possible.

Also, thank you, John Legg and Alex Wilson, for technical rescues when the computer got the huff.

I am indebted to Rev Patrick Helyer for the two photographs of horses being swum across the creek at Port San Carlos. I am indebted to the Falkland Island Company for allowing me to use their photograph of R.M.S. Darwin at sea.

For any acknowledgements overlooked, my sincere apologies.

E. J. Colgate

GLOSSARY

The {bracketed} pronunciation aids are for how I thought the word was said. The (') means, stress the next syllable; like 'penny, not pe-'nee.

albatross: Those seen from Darwin were Wandering Albatross, wing span 3m. The Black-browed, span 2½m, nests in the Falklands.

balsam bog: {'ballsum}A plant; grows as hard mound of close branchlets.

bastos: {'bas-toes} Used instead of a saddle, it comprises two leather pieces hinged with straps. At each end is a slightly raised pommel.

Beaver: A De Havilland float plane. It can carry 6 or 7 passengers.

beef quota: Live cattle that a farm has to send to Stanley for beef.

bit: Shaped, metal piece put in horse's mouth and attached to reins.

black list: People banned from buying or consuming alcohol.

bogged: Vehicle or animal that has become immobile in soft ground.

bolas: {'bo-las} Used to catch geese. Three lengths of cord, centrally knotted, equally weighted at two ends with lighter weight at the third.

bozal: {ba-'zal} Head harness for horse when it is caught. [Excludes bit.]

bun: Any sort of small cake.

cabresto: {ca-'bres-toe} The leading rein attached to the bozal.

Camp: Anywhere in the Falkland Islands outside Stanley.

cast: A sheep on its back and unable to regain its feet.

cincha: {sinch} The strap round the horse to keep bastos secure.

cojinillo: {'co-ca-'nesia} Woolly sheepskin on bastos; secured by cincha.

cut: A group of animals separated from the main group.

diddle-dee: Small leaved shrub with edible red berries. It burns easily.

dip: Immerse the sheep in a formulated solution to kill parasites.

fencing: Erect fences of wire strands tensioned to large wooden posts.

firebird: A type of petrel, the slender-billed prion. It has an inverted W on each wing. In flight, it makes rapid changes of direction .

Gentoo: A species of penguin common in the Falkland Islands. It lays two eggs. If either is taken, the Gentoo will lay another.

hydroponic: A system where plants are cultivated without soil. The necessary nutrients and growing conditions are carefully controlled.

logger: The Falkland Islands flightless steamer duck.

maletas: {ma-'lay-tuss} A pair of strong canvas bags carried across the saddle. Long flaps keep contents dry.

maori coat: Heavy, waterproof canvas coat which is also wind proof.

Montevideo: Capital port of Uruguay 1000 miles north of Stanley.

navvy: A farm worker who is not a shepherd. A navvy can undertake sheep work and be part of the shearing gang.

outside house: A shepherd's house, away from the farm settlement and usually miles from any other house, situated so that the shepherd is closer to the sheep he is responsible for.

palenque: {pa-'lenky} A large wooden framework, open to the weather, from which a complete beef carcass can be hung safe from dogs.

peat: Partially carbonized vegetation. Cut into sods by spade in spring as cuboids and built into a low lattice work to allow the wind to blow between the sods and dry them before they are carted to the house.

petrel: A sea-bird. There are several species in the Falkland Islands.

race: The narrow enclosure where an animal can be kept immobilized.

R/T: Receiver/transmitter radio telephone. An operator can switch from receive to transmit but not have both modes operative at once.

scow: Barge carried on deck of ships making a cargo trip round the islands; used if shallow water obliges the ship to anchor offshore.

separator: A machine to divide cream from milk by centrifugal force.

settlement: Where the farm manager and most farm workers live.

shedders: Geese that have moulted their flight feathers.

skua: A sea-bird that takes eggs, young geese, penguins and lambs.

smoko: The morning/afternoon short break for tea or coffee and a bun.

sod: The dried, spade-blade size, block of peat. It is chopped to a suitable size; small for quick, constant heat, large for slow burning.

stone-run: Formations, in varying width, of rocks down mountain.

tea-berry; Low plant; sweet flavoured berry; leaves once used as tea.

tick: The ked, a wingless fly. A harmful parasite on sheep.

Town: Stanley; and only Stanley.

turned: An egg where the young bird is developing.

tussac grass: A valued grass for winter fodder. Grows as tall clumps.

two metre set: V.H.F. radio-telephone on the two metre wave band.

two-nighter: Social weekend gathering including two evening dances that traditionally continue well into the small hours.

vanilla daisy: Found only in the Falklands. Its scent is vanilla.

white grass: The most common Falklands grass; not a quality grass.

wigging: Trimming facial wool on sheep to prevent wool blindness.

THE FALKLAND ISLANDS

PLACES VISITED ARE
DENOTED BY [V]

OTHER PLACES

1 Paloma Sands
2 The Moro
3 New House of Glamis
4 Moss Side
5 Cerro Montevideo
6 Third Corral Shanty
7 The Verde
8 Wreck Point
9 Head of the Bay
10 Docherty's Shanty
11 Mount Usborne

PREFACE

During the sixties, I had three unforgettable years as a travelling teacher in the Falkland Islands, moving at fortnightly intervals around farms where there were families with children of school age.

The Falklands countryside may not be magnificently awe inspiring but it has a special attraction of its own with boulder strewn mountain sides, peat pocked hill tops, stream riddled valleys and shorelines of pure white sand. It has grey days of low, rain sodden cloud, days of bright, warm sunshine and days of a tireless wind.

In the nineteenth century, men created farms on this landscape. Sheep, cows and horses joined the native seals and penguins.

Each farm covered thousands of acres divided into extensive paddocks for sheep. The farm settlement, where the manager and farm employees lived, was small. A few of the shepherd families lived in scattered 'outside' houses miles from a neighbour. Their transport was the horse. The horse still ruled supreme in the 1960's.

Spring, summer and autumn brought long hours for everyone; shepherd, navvy, manager and housewife. Winter allowed more time for social life with its crowning glory, the 'two-nighter' dance when visitors rode across from neighbouring farms.

Here are the ups and downs of life with limited facilities and communications. The story of a resourceful people imbued with a generous hospitality both warm-hearted and sincere.

The final chapter moves forward through letters from islanders during the 1982 conflict to the great changes of recent years which have brought the Falkland Islands into the 21st century.

Children of the book have long reached adulthood. Parents have become proud grandparents. Inevitably, some have passed away.

E.J.Colgate

CUTTING THE THREAD

A week before Christmas 1958, the Royal Mail Ship Darwin, freshly painted in lilac and white, steamed out of Montevideo Harbour. At anchor, she had seemed more tug than ship when viewed from the deck of a liner ten times her size. Now she was the life-line to the Falkland Islands with mail, essential cargo and a full booking of passengers.

As she left the shelter of the River Plate and met the swell of the open ocean, she began her hall-mark roll, a continuous, monotonous motion with never a moment's respite.

For the first hours, there was company; tankers, small coasters and fishing boats. Anonymous gauze-winged insects in shiny ruby and green buzzed the ship. A slender lemon-breasted bird landed on the rail, stayed a while and flew off again.

By evening, Darwin was on her own, queen of the southern seas, heading home towards Port Stanley. Few other ships would head that way; just the chartered wool-boat, the Royal Navy Patrol Ship and survey vessels for the Antarctic bases.

That night as I was rocked disconcertingly towards sleep, I wondered where the roll would take us if the sea became rough and what on earth I was doing aboard an unstable little ship, heading for islands I had barely heard about in order to spend three years travelling around sheep farms as a school teacher.

The next day, when sea sickness obliged me to rush from the lunch table, I knew violently across the rail that I had no wish to be aboard any ship.

The feeling passed with the tomato soup, it had been an early exit. A tablet and warm sunshine soon adjusted things. On deck, a centrally placed seat minimized the ship's movement and a somnolent murmur from the funnel induced a peaceful sleep.

When I awoke, the drowsiness remained and the seat seemed too comfortable a place to vacate. A small shadow flicked across the deck as a swallow glided by and settled on the boat. It stayed preening itself, resting for over an hour before flying off. The last mainland thread was cut.

The sky was left to the seabirds; the albatross with its fascinating mastery of the air, the wave-clinging petrel and the ephemeral, chevron-winged firebird appearing and disappearing as it changed direction. Across the waves, spouting whales fountain-frothed and descended into the echoes of the ship's throbbing engines.

The sea kept calm, no more than a gentle swell. Darwin's roll lost its significance and the voyage became peacefully pleasant; good food, a comfortable cabin and cheerful company.

At noon on the third day the ship's log showed we had another 334 miles to pass in chatter, cards and rolling deck exercise as afternoon stretched to evening and a last bunk-rocking night aboard.

The new day dawned with a thick sea mist. Darwin's wake bubbled white and straight astern but the mist clung to it, clutching at the ship as it rolled nowhere and back again in a narrow ocean devoid of any view.

Passengers could do no more than talk the time away. They discussed wool prices and shearing yet again, appraised the seasonal cocktail parties of Government House, took sides in championing the merits of West or East Falkland horses and jockeys at race meetings, reviewed the winter's sheepdog trials and laughed over the perils of dancing 'two-nighters in Camp'. The islands seemed to have a special way of life.

By lunchtime, homeward-bound passengers were in festive mood. Within hours they would be in Port Stanley.

An afternoon sun nudged overhead, nibbling the mist and expanding the sea. People were alert, peering hopefully forward.

"There!" an excited voice.

"Where?"

A grey smudge lay on the horizon.

The lounge cleared. Passengers crowded the ship's rail. Those returning home waited for a magic outline to build. A few still wondered what lay ahead.

Gradually, a shoreline took shape; the Falkland Islands.

Sunshine flecked the waves but the islands remained almost colourless, white grassed hills with the faintest touch of lichen-green.

Cormorants formed an escort, black winged, solemn and unwavering. Surf broke white against the shore. Dark water marked an inlet. Darwin turned to starboard between two headlands into a narrowing waterway.

1: R.M.S. Darwin in calm waters.

She no longer rolled. Slowly she passed rich green tussac-grass islets and a splattering of wave-washed rocks with a lighthouse standing sentinel on the shore. Seals slid from a rock. To one side an old, stump-masted wreck stood forlorn in a bay, her days of Victorian glory forgotten. On the other side were sand dunes, crystal-white humped and tumbled sand and a pair of ducks threshing furiously across the water with frantic wing beats that created spumes of spray yet failed to give the birds flight.

"Loggers," explained an islander noting my amusement. "They try like crazy but never get airborne."

Slower and still slower Darwin crept until just the tide seemed to be drifting her on. A last turn and a glory of man-made colour stood stacked along the hillside. Port Stanley, with neat, bright white houses, red-roofed, green-roofed in welcoming rows and the evening sun glinting, flicking gold off the windows. Blue-grey smoke curled from chimneys and a strange but attractive scent lay in the air, peat smoke, subtle and comforting, a promise of fireside and friendly hearth.

Amid a jangle of engine room bells R.M.S. Darwin nosed alongside a short jetty.

No fussy tugs, no bevy of hooting whistles. No huge cranes. No stream of dockers, officials and police. Just a few simple formalities.

Islanders came aboard and were welcoming friends. Somebody introduced himself to me, bidding welcome to the Falklands.

"Buzz Aldridge will run you up to your lodgings. You'll be very comfortable there with Nanna King. Nanna's a great person. She will tell you all you need to know, and more besides once she gets chatting. Your trunk will be up tomorrow. Cheerio."

Buzz Aldridge led me to a Land Rover. It was a short drive up the hill from the jetty, turn left, bump along pot-holed Fitzroy Road and stop at the gate of 49. I climbed a long flight of steps up the garden to a neat conservatory ablaze with crimson geraniums. There stood Nanna King welcoming me at the door.

Nanna smiled and burst into words, "Here you are then. We watched the boat coming in. It's a nice view across the harbour from here. The other boat there's the John Biscoe. She's been down south to the Antarctic bases. This is my other lodger, John. He was a Camp teacher too out on the West. Now what do we call you?"

"Ted," was my contribution to the conversation.

"Well, Ted, I'm Nanna. Now you need a good supper. It's mutton tonight. I hope you like mutton. We call it 365. You'll soon work out why. I'll be busy in the kitchen now so I'll leave you with John."

"Hi, Ted. Welcome to the Falklands. They're a fine people out here. I'm from the States but this is my home now. After supper we'll have a walk round Stanley."

ISLAND CAPITAL

We did not see quite all of Stanley that evening but next morning we comfortably completed the tour.

Stanley, 'Town' to the islanders, was the capital of the Falklands. Just over 1000 people lived there; half the population of the islands. No other place matched it for size, status or facilities. Outside Town you were in Camp, be it East or West Falkland or the smaller islands; no roads, no villages, no signposts, just Camp with sheep, scenery and settlements.

Nobody would start comparing Stanley with capitals like London, Edinburgh or Cardiff. To do so would be ludicrous. Yet comparison with a British village of a thousand inhabitants would be equally ludicrous. What village had a cathedral, a legislature, a treasury, a magistrates' court and prison, a hospital, a power station, a meteorological office, a water works, a Volunteer Defence Force, a broadcasting station, an airport and a racecourse; or a galvanized roof on practically every house? Stanley was unique.

From the cemetery in the east to Government House in the west was about a mile and from the shoreline inland was less than ½ a mile. Within that rectangle lay virtually everything.

The beach was a low tide exposure of rock. Along the shore were half a dozen jetties of varying small sizes. Out in the harbour a four masted barque, Fennia, gave an olde worlde touch to the scene. She had been the victim of a Cape Horn storm and had limped back to Stanley to become a storage hulk. Other more decrepit hulks formed part of some jetties, and timbers from old sailing ships did duty ashore as fences and outbuildings.

The roads had been laid in a grid system with plenty of space between for the houses. The road surfaces varied. A few were good; some were abysmal.

2: Stanley Cathedral, with the Fennia hulk in the harbour.

For most people, cars were not a necessity but for some of the elderly residents a neighbourly car lift was the only way they could hope to get around. The most practical vehicle was the Land Rover which was able to tackle rough tracks and open country as well as the town's criss-cross of tarmac streets.

The oldest houses were a short row of detached cottages erected in 1850. A terrace of four brick-built, bay-windowed houses on the front could have belonged to an Edwardian seaside resort but the normal materials were wood and metal sheeting which, like most things, had been imported.

The varied designs and sizes of the buildings prevented any monotony. Some had square sash-cord windows flanking a central front door and bedrooms set high beneath the roof. Others had wide bay windows and a conservatory that was both porch and flower garden.

The main gardens were largely given over to vegetables. Only the industrious gardener could have dependable fresh produce to accompany the mutton, mutton, mutton meat which dominated the diet of everyone.

Cooking and heating were almost entirely fuelled by peat. This was cut at the banks on the hills behind the town, left to dry in the ever dependable wind and then carted home by lorry.

Shops were well distributed. The Philomel Store, built in yellow vertical corrugated sheeting beside the main jetty, offered the 'best' of everything. If Des, the jovial proprietor, could not persuade you his item was just what you needed, he extended his cheerful farewell with an invitation for you to call again if you changed your mind. Des was ever the optimist.

The long, solid Falkland Islands Company's West Store was functionally fine but the formality of its displays lacked the jumbled intimacy of some smaller shops. In the Company Store you felt everything was being conducted with a faultless and time honoured propriety fashioned in a time when nothing was meant to change.

The Globe Store hinted at the world wide source of goods in town. There was no pandering to the U.K. in the eyes of Stanley shopkeepers. Free trade and no embargoes: Germany and Japan for cameras and radios, Norway for winter warmth, England for cornflakes.

There was one eye-catching monument, the whale bone arch of four great curving jaw bones. It had neat beds of marigolds around it and, dependent upon your position, it framed the cathedral or a well proportioned house or part of the harbour.

The Church of England Cathedral was an imposing Victorian stone building, rugged more than graceful, with decorative red brick around the arched windows and in the buttressed tower. The Roman Catholic Chapel and the Non-conformist Tabernacle provided for spiritual needs equally well in smaller buildings that blended with their surroundings. Congregations were not great but padre, priest and minister were always ready to help and kept an open door for anyone in need.

The pubs did not keep such open doors although the spirit was willing. Licensed drinking hours were strictly observed. On Sunday the only permitted time was the Glory Hour before dinner. For the rest of the sabbath they remained firmly closed.

The clubs had more generous drinking times. In them one could drink beyond the heart's content. A person who over imbibed, and drink was an easy companion on the islands, could be put on the Black List which would ban him from all drink for a specified time. A few went to the length of putting themselves on the list to try to break their addiction.

Sport provided for all who were interested. Most popular was football which was a summer game organised as a small league. The pitch was at the western extremity of the town. It was not level, it could not be level in Stanley, but it did have a well drained playing surface.

Beyond the football pitch was the racecourse, complete with covered stand, where the annual meeting took place each Christmas. John took me along on Boxing Day.

It was a day out for everyone. As we approached, an aura of cheerful bonhomie enveloped us. For many it seemed a time to chat with friends from Camp, for some it was a chance to participate in the athletics and fun events which laced the race programme, for others it was the perfect occasion to relax and watch.

Everybody knew the jockeys who were shepherds, clerks or shop-girls for most days but became brightly silked riders for race day. When the loud-speakers announced each forthcoming race, jockeys and horses made their way to the start and the crowd gathered expectantly at the finish. Eyes were turned along the course.

The starter's signal went and the horses ran. The jockeys rode hard. There was a race to be won. Go man go, was the call with no quarter asked or given. At the end, it was glory for some, winnings for the backers and for the others another try shortly when Lady Luck might be more favourable.

The meeting concluded with the Race Dance in the Town Hall, a well attended and extremely enjoyable evening.

Next night we stayed at home to listen to the local radio station broadcasting reports and interviews of the meeting. Listening to the descriptions was almost like reliving the events.

The Falkland Islands Broadcasting Service was on the air every evening and the dedicated staff put out a well varied programme from their somewhat cramped studio.

Another building noteworthy for achievement if not for its beauty was the 27-bed Edward VII Memorial Hospital. It was the birthplace of most young islanders.

The Stanley babies in due course took their place at the cuboid infant school. The Senior School had more character and was where most children completed their schooling.

The administrative offices of the education department were housed in an insipid white block. There the director controlled affairs. To him I went to be briefed on my teaching area. Hopes of being sent to West Falkland Island or the small outer islands were quickly dashed. So many had extolled the virtues and glories of the West that being assigned to East Falkland came as a blow. It was to be two farms, San Carlos and Port San Carlos, in the north-west corner of the island.

Back at Nanna's John would listen to no complaints. He assured me the San Carloses were attractive settlements surrounded by hills very similar to those on the West and far more scenic than the low, pond-dotted southern part of East Falkland. Furthermore, being on the West was excellent as long as inter-island transport was operating but difficulties arose when the plane was out of service or the winds were too high for flying. The San Carloses, he maintained, were splendid places.

Say what John may, when the radio announcements after the news included my name on the flight list, I felt a slight twinge at leaving the homeliness of Nanna King's house to set off for somewhere strange again.

Beaver Hopping to San Carlos

Flight day was hot with a steady breeze. I was taken by Land Rover along another pot-holed roadway to the creek-side hangar a mile or so west of the town.

The Air Service comprised two De Haviland Beaver Seaplanes each carrying five or six passengers. One plane had just taken off. The other floated beside a concrete ramp.

Luggage was put aboard and passengers' names were called. We shuffled along the wide float, climbed two steep rungs to the cabin and squeezed into our allotted seats. Squeeze it was, for the plane had a full load. The pilot ascertained that all was well in the cabin, settled himself at the controls and switched on. The engine came to life. Slowly we crossed the narrow creek. The pilot turned into wind, paused for flight clearance and began take-off.

The plane roared back across the water, spray lashing the side windows and lifted into free air. The hangar was left further and further below. The bends of the blue creek became patterned in the grassy countryside. The narrow well-worn mud track became a wriggled line in brown crayon smudged in places where cattle grazed by its side. The shallow valleys, white-grassed tangles of small streams and peaty ponds, seemed devoid of life. The plane rose clear of the surrounding hills which seemed like cushions of green sponge inset with pumice-stone where rocky outcrops capped the summits.

On the left, was a line of higher mountains. They were smeared with 'stone runs', petrified cascades of boulders from past geological ages, as if cans of grey-white paint had been tipped down the mountain sides. At the far end of the range, Mount Usborne shouldered above the rest, the highest peak in the islands.

Far to the right were the heavy indentations of the coast running into a large promontory and returning to form the Falkland Sound

3: The Beaver swoops low over San Carlos wool shed to the creek.

separating the two main islands. On the horizon were the mountains of West Falkland.

After 20 minutes of rather bumpy flight, the pilot told us we were approaching San Carlos. Below us, was a small group of red and white houses beside a creek.

The plane banked sharply, lost height as it swept over the houses, straightened out across the water and made a smooth landing in the bay. It taxied to a small raft.

A boat was rowed out from a wooden jetty. Outgoing and incoming mails were exchanged. The two passengers for San Carlos, a young girl and myself, transferred to the rowing boat. The plane taxied away and the boat returned to the jetty.

George, the retiring teacher, was waiting there. We walked up the jetty along a length of narrow-gauge railway which seemed totally out of place until George explained its purpose in running a small trolley laden with wool-bales when the charter boat called. A short way above the jetty was a large yellow building, the wool-shed, the working heart of San Carlos.

George took me to a semi-detached house, the home of Christine

4: Early morning at San Carlos settlement.

and Charles with their two sons, Ron and Gerald, where I was to stay for the next fortnight. It was 'smoko' time when everyone broke for a cup of tea and a bun. Christine poured me tea and offered cakes as if I had lived there all my life. After smoko, Gerald, 13 and in his final year at school, gave me a guided tour of the settlement.

On the neatly-kept green were two more houses, a community hall with a small school at one end, a fenced area enclosing vegetable gardens and a two-storied building that could have been flats but was the cookhouse where the single men each had a room. A gorse-hedged track led to the manager's Big House and, a little beyond it, the cowman/gardener's house set in a well kept garden with a crunchy, white shell path to the door. Close beside every house was a fly-proof meat-safe and a carefully constructed stack of peat sods. San Carlos, population 23; home, workplace and leisure centre week by week through the seasons of the year.

After dinner, George took me to the school. It consisted of a classroom big enough for eight or ten children, a store-room planned as a bed-sit for a permanent teacher and a cloakroom. The school roll comprised Gerald, his seven year old neighbour, Heather, and

Patrick, just five, from the house with the white shell path. Their two weeks school term would be followed by eight weeks of homework.

George pointed across the creek to a small white lozenge on the opposite shore where I would one day be teaching. It was Wreck Point, home of John, the farm's head shepherd, and his family, one of four outside houses located so that all parts of the farm could be properly shepherded.

Also on the creek-side not far from Wreck Point was the Ajax Bay Freezer plant, built as an outlet for Falkland mutton. It had cost almost half a million pounds to build but insufficient suitable meat was received and after two years it had ceased functioning. Just the main building remained and a caretaker had the lonely task of keeping an eye on the place.

For Wreck Point people to reach the settlement entailed a ride around Head of the Bay at the top of the creek. Over the hills beyond Head of the Bay was Sussex. Three boys awaited me there. For those children, term time would be two weeks in every sixteen. No children lived at the last of the outside houses, The Verde, which was somewhere behind the hills at the back of the settlement.

The information was an eye opener. San Carlos was not just the settlement and surrounding fields at all. According to George, there were over 60,000 acres of San Carlos spread beyond the mountains both behind us and across the creek. Scattered around it, were 24,000 sheep. The tiny Falklands suddenly seemed vast.

Bed that evening was early as the next day would also begin early with Christine off to milk her cows and Charles and Ron at work by six. The bed was comfortable and I was quickly asleep but the new day's dawn began at four and then sound sleep was gone. I raised myself on one arm to peer out of the window.

The view at that hour was indistinct. San Carlos lay cloaked by night shadow which merged with the hill slopes to form a high wall enclosing the settlement and isolating it. A cow lowed mournfully. On the green below the window a dog nosed something, gnawed it a moment and discarded it, a sheep's skull. A sheep's skull in a lonely valley cut off from the world by a black mountain wall. If ever three years seemed a long time, they seemed it then.

By breakfast, life was in better perspective. It was a sunny morning, the skull had been cleared away and the green was tidy again. Outside, a strong wind gusted off the creek fanning the feathers of the hens pecking round the peat stacks. Inside, mutton chops and fried goose egg were on a warm plate, a slice of home-made bread to one side and a mug of steaming coffee to the other. The chops were excellent but the first impression of wild goose egg was of a somewhat grassy taste.

The radio was tuned to 4.5 megs for the morning 'R/T' messages which passed between Stanley and the farm managers. Each farm had its R/T, receiver/transmitter set, and scheduled air times when the manager or his wife would respond to the call from Stanley. The R/Ts were compulsive breakfast time listening for almost every household and the voice of Syd Summers, the Stanley operator, was familiar to everyone.

Bleaker Island, one of the dozen or so smaller inhabited islands, was being called, "Stanley calling Bleaker, Stanley calling Bleaker. Over."

"Bleaker answering Stanley. Good morning Syd ......"

Messages were exchanged and a store shopping order made. Bleaker signed off and the next farm was called.

Some of the West Falkland farms provided weather reports. These were of special interest to people booked to fly because they gave some indication of the possibility of flights taking place; strong winds could make the creeks too rough for safe operating.

Strong winds could also be too high for the wind chargers which recharged the 6 or 12 volt batteries necessary for the house lighting and power. Too much or too little wind could mean no light and no radio. If the wind failed for too long, light was provided by Tilley lamp. The Tilley needed preheating by a special 'torch' soaked in methylated spirit. When the meths had heated the mantle and the lamp had been pumped to the proper pressure, Tilley light was efficient but it could not revive a faded radio; only the wind could do that.

On the R/Ts San Carlos was referred to as JB to distinguish it from Port San Carlos, known as KC. These were the owners' initials

5: Charles' wind charger by his house. Big John has the other semi-detached.

and had been as good a way as any to minimize confusion.

Needless to say, confusion did occur. George, by being a Smith, unwittingly instigated one such occasion. As a travelling teacher he sometimes needed to move books from one farm to another. A few weeks before my arrival he wanted to shift several bulky bundles from Port San Carlos to San Carlos. Although the farms were next door to each other, the settlements were separated by an arm of the creek and two hill ridges. The best way to transport heavy items between the two places was by boat.

George had put his books in the charge of a friend aboard R.M.S. Darwin which was calling at both farms on its December Camp trip. Unfortunately Darwin arrived at Port San Carlos on a Saturday. Saturday was always store-day when the settlement shop opened for the sale of provisions to the housewife and when men could purchase their weekly half-bottle of spirits, usually whisky, gin or rum.

George's friend had bought his bottle and enjoyed it with his companions so that he was rather cheerful when the ship left. He completely forgot his mission and the bundle, not being labelled, was landed at Port Howard on West Falkland.

George eventually traced the whereabouts of his books and

arranged through the post office to have them shifted back when Darwin made her January Camp trip.

In January, Darwin reached Port Howard as scheduled. Next was San Carlos.

That morning, George sat at breakfast, possibly listening to the R/Ts, possibly simply aware of them as background noise. West Point's weather report was given and flights seemed probable. A number of messages had passed to and fro between Stanley and the Camp stations when Mr Cameron at Port San Carlos came on the air.

"Hello, Stanley, Hello, Stanley. This is KC calling Stanley. Over."

"Come in KC. Over."

"Syd, good morning to you. Syd, I gather that a Mr Smith has asked for a load of something or other to be shifted over from Port Howard. Well, there is only one Mr Smith in Port San Carlos and whatever it is, it does not belong to him. Can you help, Syd? Over"

"Hello KC. Yes, I've got that. I'll see what I can do. Over."

George, immediately alert, began to "tut-tut" and twitch in his seat anxious about his books. Inter-island surface mail was more a monthly than a weekly service and certainly not a daily one. Nor did air-freight rates encourage bulky items.

A few more messages were passed then Stanley was calling KC again, sorry that he could not help and promising to call Port Howard.

Another voice joined in, "Hello, Stanley. Howard calling. Over"

"Hello, Port Howard. Go ahead. Over."

"Hello Stanley. Well, that was the message I received from the Post Office but if the things are nothing to do with Port San Carlos I'll not bother to send them. Over."

Port San Carlos voiced agreement and got off the air. George, for his part, was out of the door, racing up the green towards the Big House as if half the settlement dogs were at him.

After a minute or so of silence, Port Howard came back with a solution, "Hello, Stanley. We seem to have solved the puzzle. I'm told there's a Smith further across on West Point. The stuff must be his. I'll arrange to shift it to him. Over."

Bursting across this tentative solution came the clear, booming voice of Mr Bonner, the San Carlos manager, "Hello, Howard. Hello,

Howard. This is JB calling Howard. A distraught teacher has just arrived at my house. Those goods are for him here at San Carlos and he doesn't fancy going to West Point for them. We need them here at San Carlos. Sorry about the muddle. Out."

Thanks to the manager's timely intervention, George's books arrived safely that evening with Darwin. The incident was over.

San Carlos preferred to keep off the air as much as possible as the settlement was linked to Stanley by telephone. Stanley had a comprehensive network although the phones were of a magneto type which necessitated whirring a handle to ring the operator who would then obtain the requisite number.

The link between East Falkland settlements was not so good. San Carlos was on the end of a single line that also served several other settlements and some outside houses as well. Obtaining Stanley was a complicated procedure of whirring the ringing code for Camilla Creek, the next house along the line, who would ring a further house who then might be able to ring the Stanley operator for you. If the people at one vital house were out, the whole process could break down and it became a case of try again later and again, and again. Even so, JB preferred the phone to the very public R/T conversations and left others to provide the breakfast entertainment on 4.5 megs.

AND SO TO HORSE

The fortnight passed. It was time to move across to Port San Carlos; time for the introduction to riding. I was to have Roy, a docile brown old horse which had served the shepherds well and was now used only for occasions such as the present when a quiet tame mount was required. George was guide and would attend to the 'handing-over' ceremonies at KC.

The simple theory of Falkland Island riding had been explained the previous evening. The one important riding difference between the Falklands and Britain was the method of steering. The horses were shepherds' horses and the shepherds rode the South American gaucho way; a hand for the horse and a hand for work. So the reins were held in one hand and the horse was guided by pushing the reins against the opposite side of the horse's neck to the direction you wished to go. This could be confusing to those used to riding in Britain but since I had never ridden before it would not affect my horsemanship.

There seemed to be a considerable language barrier when it came to the naming of parts. The horse-gear terms recalled the gaucho days. A bozal was slipped over the horse's head when you caught it and the leading rein was the cabresto. Instead of a saddle, there were bastos, two leather pieces hinged with straps and having slight pommels at each end. The bastos were topped by a thick sheepskin, the cojinillo that gave the competent rider a very comfortable seat. The girth

6: A horse with bastos instead of saddle.

7: Keith comfortable on the sheepskin cojinillo.

was called the cincha. Finally there was a pair of maneas for hobbling the front feet if necessary. The bit, the reins, the stirrups and the rug managed to keep English.

George also explained that there was no ethical requirement for the rider to post up and down in style when trotting. However, he omitted the simple first rule that one geared the horse, mounted, dismounted and ungeared it always from the left side of the animal. George had yet to find how inept a rider he had on his hands.

Moving time entailed luggage as well; essential clothing, personal comforts and teaching paraphernalia. Packing was no 'throw it in a case' affair but a skill to be acquired gradually through constant fortnightly moves. Everything had to be fitted into a pair of canvas pannier bags, the maletas, slung across the saddle. It was imperative that the two sides balanced. George ensured they did.

Although on most days the wind had risen with the sun, moving day was reasonably calm. Roy stood geared and patient by the garden fence. I too was geared in blue dungarees, a pair of Chilean riding boots a size too large and a ruck-sack containing a macintosh in case of rain. A maori coat of heavy proofed canvas was the normal protective garment but that had yet to be purchased. The maori was carried rolled up and tied across the back of the saddle so that it could be put on quickly when rain squalls threatened.

Both horses were ready. It was time to mount. I thrust one foot into the stirrup, grabbed hold of the saddle and heard George say, "Ahem! Ted, one usually holds the reins."

Abashed at overlooking the obvious, I adjusted my grip to include the reins, pretended the horse was a bicycle and mounted.

For a small horse, Roy kept his rider amazingly high from the ground. Falling off might be painful. Roy began to move away, a gentle walk down the slope towards the creek. Tentative pulling on the reins did not seem to deter him. He reached the hedge of the foreman's garden and stopped.

George too had mounted and set off in some other direction. I was not sure where because I had my back to him and did not fancy twisting round to see. Roy sampled the hedge, munched a few leaves and then, having established his authority, he turned of his own accord and wandered after George.

George was waiting at a gate leading to the peat banks, a jumble of workings where the peat had been cut for years past. We threaded our way through them to the foot of the first hill. The lower slopes were gentle and George set his horse at a trot. Roy walked off in a different direction. George waited patiently until we met up again. Gradually the hill became steeper and George announced that we would have to zigzag which was what Roy had more or less been doing since the peat banks.

Zigzag it was and while George's horse steadily ascended the hill, Roy seemed to gain little height at all. An occasional sheep looked at us. Once or twice a small bird rose from the grass to alight again out of our path. There did not seem to be any flowers; just grass, a few rocks, a glitter of water where a small stream flowed down and dull olive patches of shrubby diddle-dee. The creek looked a rich blue. Wreck Point house showed clear on the far side. Roy plodded to and fro methodically. San Carlos settlement became small white matchboxes. Above me, at the top of the hill, George was waiting, as patient as ever, sitting against a convenient rock while his horse grazed the white grass.

At last, Roy reached the top. The rock looked exceedingly inviting and I was certainly ready for the rest.

Not so. George mounted again anxious to continue. We had, he stated, been in the saddle an hour, a reasonable time for the ride except that we had covered only a third of it. He indicated the way across a wide valley and declared the ground was firm enough for trotting.

George trotted away. Roy seemed content to walk so I jiggled the reins hopefully. My hopes were realized and Roy just kept walking. George threw a few hints over his shoulder.

"Dig your heels in." No result.

"You've got to show him who's boss." I was satisfied the way things were.

"Give him a whack on the flank," George's voice was becoming distinctly more distant in both space and tone.

"No thanks," I called and continued my progress. Ahead, George halted and watched. He waited as Roy and I approached.

"You carry on, Ted," said George, so I, ever gullible, sat contentedly as Roy walked by.

"Whack!" George smote him across the hind quarters. Roy went. With hoofs pounding and the white grass streaming past, he whirled me away in a mad gallop.

'Oh agony! Hold the reins and clasp the saddle. Did a cowboy ever go so fast?'

Fortunately, Roy soon took stock of the situation and recomposed himself. He slowed to an uncomfortable trot until we reached a shallow brook.

During our ride so far there had been little to indicate we were on a regular track but at the brook the banks were worn and hoof prints marked the mud. Roy stepped unhesitatingly in and waded across to mid-stream where he uncompromisingly jerked the reins from my grasp, lowered his head and began to drink. Peering down his neck was disquieting. I knew I was about to slide down it at any second. I could feel my body being slowly edged forward by some unseen force. The outcome seemed inevitable but Roy had no great thirst. He raised his neck again. We completed the crossing and recommenced the trotting experience.

To minimise discomfort I gripped with my knees and attempted to jog up and down on Roy's back while the ruck-sack jogged up and down on mine. The horse and ruck-sack seemed to find a respectable rhythm and I bumped down on the off beat. Eventually, the second hill was reached and slowly ascended.

From the top we could see the Port San Carlos arm of the creek with the narrow double-turn by the settlement which lay back out of sight on the further shore.

The horses knew their journey was almost finished and needed no coaxing down the hill and around to the headland by the creek. There I pulled on the reins and Roy obediently halted. Happily I swung my foot over the saddle and slithered to the ground on the wrong side of the horse in a final act of unhorsemanship.

"Not that side, Ted, or you'll land yourself in trouble." Quite prophetic words.

George hobbled the horses to prevent them wandering. We took the gear off Roy and put it with the maletas by the creekside to await the boat already being rowed across for us.

The keel ground against the shore. We handed my gear and maletas aboard and clambered on. The rower pushed off again, poled the boat through a thick brown mass of kelp weed and began to row.

Once ashore, there remained a ten minutes' walk to the next fortnight's home with Bill and Clara and their three children. The hour's journey had taken two and a half.

George looked back across the creek and gave a heartfelt sigh. His hobbled horse was courageously making for home up the far hillside. George would not have a quick journey back.

8: Looking back to the creek on the way to Bill and Clara's at Port San Carlos.

Down in the Valley

Port San Carlos settlement had been built along the valley stretching parallel with the creek towards the Falkland Sound. Several small streams drained the valley and merged to flow to the beach in the little back-cut bay.

Just above the shore line stood the Victorian cookhouse, nearly 100 years old. With white painted weather-boarding and red gabled roof, it had an air of established dignity. The rooms were low and dark with the upper ones set in the roof, two towards the creek and two towards the settlement. It was the focal point of social life at Port San Carlos, the venue for dances, the weekly film and the winter whist drives.

Along the low hill between the settlement and the creek was a small sand quarry where the men sometimes dug out fossils of shell fish. Beyond the quarry there was a veritable maze of interconnected squares hedged by thick gorse bushes. These provided shelter for freshly shorn sheep when successive rain squalls swept through the valley, a possibility even in summer. Above the gorse squares, was a small, fenced area; the cemetery. There were few graves and it was many years since the last burial but the cemetery remained a hallowed place.

The hills on the inward side rose 200 metres to the angularly stacked Settlement Rocks standing cracked and weather-crumbled across the skyline. From there, wonderful panoramas were spread wide on a wind that seldom ceased until the sun set, the views shrank and a peaceful quiet stole across the landscape as long twilight shadows became night.

On a calm spring day, the scent of the gorse squares in full flower saturated the hillside air and bewitched it. Port San Carlos became a jewel in its valley, canopied by yellow gorse, washed by the blue creek

1: San Carlos. Charles rows out to collect passengers arriving on the Beaver.

2: San Carlos. Looking across the settlement to cloud-capped Fanning Head
and the Falkland Sound.

3: Bill's house at Port San Carlos. In the background are the West Falkland mountains.

4: The view from the Settlement Rocks across Port San Carlos to Mount Usborne.

5: Cape Dolphin. Muzzie makes the most of the weather to milk outside.

6: Jenny separates the cream from the milk;
cream for butter, milk for the cows.

7: Stan and Rab cart home the peat at Cape Dolphin. After being cut, it dried in the wind.

8: Muzzie knits in the rocking chair. Jenny keeps warm. In front of the fire is Stan's rag mat.

and backed in the distance by Mount Usborne ruling the hills around it.

Down in the valley, the fragrance of gorse counted for nothing. The real essence of life in the settlement was good neighbourliness, the way it was in all settlements. Family wellbeing depended on the understanding and good will that linked the homes in a strong bond. That the family houses and the manager's Big House straggled each side of the valley as if shunning company was of no consequence.

The last house of all was Bill and Clara's with a gaggle of tame white geese on the green, a large vegetable garden, and a view across the sound to the hills of West Falkland. Bill was head shepherd. He set himself a high standard and was never idle. He had just begun building a caravan. When finished, it would be towed to the white sands of Paloma Beach and his family would spend their days by the bay while he shepherded the ewe flock there. The base was almost complete but there were many hours of work ahead of him.

9: Bill making the family caravan. Leona, Arina and Fraser watch progress.

Bill had a quiet personality and eyes that twinkled with good humour. Clara, too, was always busy and her bubbling personality complemented Bill's perfectly. The three children had their individuality. Arina was nine, zip-full of energy and enthusiastically engrossed in the task of the moment. Leona, six, was quieter and would not be rushed. Fraser was an explosive two-year-old full of zest, eager to discover life.

In all about 40 people lived at KC. There was a wide age range from Delia, just a few months old, to Murdo and Elizabeth, parents of John at Wreck Point and Clara. Although well past retirement age, Murdo would not retire. He had been awarded the Empire Medal for his great service. His experience and knowledge were of inestimable value to the manager.

The manager's four children had a young governess so Port San Carlos, with six children of school age, had two schools. The governess taught in the sun-lounge of the Big House.

The settlement children had an old army hut in one of the paddocks. To Arina and Leona it was school, whatever its beauty or lack of it, and school meant hard work. They both worked cheerfully, were attentive and made the most of their opportunities. Mr Cameron promised a proper school room would be built once shearing was over. Since he was a man of his word the rusty hut with its cockeyed chimney was accepted.

It was usually one of the manager's children who had the honour of collecting the mail when the Beaver made an air drop. This happened when a ship arrived at Stanley with an overseas mail. As soon as the mail was ashore the post office sorted the letters. A call went out across the town radio when the sorting was complete to let people know theirs was ready for collection. Camp mail was put into special bags and the two planes incorporated mail-drops in their flight schedules for the following days.

The R/Ts provided progress reports on those flights and when Port San Carlos' turn was imminent, the manager's children were given permission to leave their lessons, find a sheltered position near the Big House lawn, the dropping zone, and await the plane's approach.

Mail-drops were always a spectacle to enjoy. If the plane was returning from a West flight, people would look for a small dot in the sky gradually shaping as it crossed the Falkland Sound. For those drops there was plenty of time to prepare. The plane dived steadily towards the settlement, zoomed low over the houses on a dummy run, banked round and returned to sweep above the lawn. From the pilot's window came the mail-bag to plummet to the ground and as the plane climbed away to its next call, the children raced to retrieve the bag.

When San Carlos was visited first, the plane would appear suddenly above the hill, be over the dropping zone and away almost before the children were out of the sun-lounge. Either way there was great rejoicing when mail arrived.

10: The Beaver heads for Douglas Station after the KC mail drop.

On three sides Port San Carlos Camp was bordered by sea. Only on the east was there a land boundary, a fence separating Douglas Station Camp. At the mouth of the creek, where occasional schools of whales spouted their spray, Fanning Head rose sharply from the water, 150 metres of rock dominating the scene. Northwards the coast became a series of low headlands with narrow beaches and bays bordered by white sand.

11: Moss Side, the home of Andreas, Orlene and Bonnie.

Sand bars had formed across some of the bays to make shallow ponds which became so warm in summer they were like bathing pools, a secluded luxury unappreciated by the penguins and seals which had their favoured locations and kept aloof.

At Foul Bay, sand-dunes marked the beginning of Cape Dolphin, the long narrowing promontory thrusting into the Atlantic. Near the beginning of the promontory was Cape Dolphin house. Much nearer the settlement, only 30 minutes ride from it, was Moss Side, the home of Andreas and Orlene.

It was to Moss Side that Clara took me at the conclusion of my two weeks at Port San Carlos. The ride was an embarrassingly laborious one perched for the first hour on Opal, a tall black mare who had no intention of taking me in even the vaguest direction of Moss Side, and then on Vamoos who resignedly plodded along while I slumped on her back painfully aware that I should be taking more a grip of myself and less so of the horse in order to make some sort of face-saving effort. At last we passed a well, turned the corner of a hill and were at the house.

Stiff-limbed and decidedly down-hearted I got off the horse and unstrapped my maletas. Andreas took my gear and I shuffled indoors.

12: Bonnie at Moss Side.

Bonnie, my prospective pupil, eyed me suspiciously. Orlene handed me a cup of tea and enquired whether I'd like one cushion or two.

Andreas and Orlene were cheerful hosts and Moss Side was a popular port of call for people riding to or from KC. There was a relaxed atmosphere and when visitors came the kitchen filled with laughter as news and stories were exchanged. When the visitors decided it was time to go and left in a flurry of dogs and horses, Moss-side settled back into its solitude and time drifted. Orlene's old house-dog kept silent vigil by the stable, the several cats lazed in the warmer corners, hens shuffled in dust baths and the only purposeful activity came from groups of gulls skirmishing around the tall wooden palenque from which the last of the beef hung.

For poor Bonnie it must have seemed that time itself was suspended. The hours were long and the days tedious. She stuck the fortnight well but was no doubt happy when teacher hauled himself aboard Waltzer to be taken away to Cape Dolphin.

BUTTER FOR THE BIG HOUSE

Andreas rode ahead along the winding valley from Moss Side. The way grew steeper until we were on a high waste land of wiry white grass and balsam, pock-marked by small dark-banked ponds where wind and rain had scoured the underlying peat. He kept steadily on although there seemed no visible track and at last we came off the hills down to the shore and through a belt of shallow water onto the white sands of a long, curving bay.

Waves rolled, broke with a crump and sighed back to the sea. Rivulets trickled after them to join the falling tide and the horses' hoofs thwacked a rhythmic pattern on the wet sand. An untidy line of half-buried vertebrae marked where, years past, a school of pilot whales had stranded themselves. Groups of sandpipers and smart chestnut-crowned plovers scurried along the sand and took occasional hurried flight to keep always a little ahead of the horses until finally flying behind again to resume their interrupted feeding. Above the high water mark the sand was powder dry and where the tussac-grass had taken root large dunes had formed.

Further along, the dunes gave way to an expanse of short cropped grass with a deep-banked stream running through. Here Andreas turned inland and followed the stream up a valley to Stan and Muzzie's house on the hill behind. There we dismounted at the stable, ungeared the horses and let them go. They rolled on the grass a few times by way of grooming, shook themselves and began feeding.

A dozen dogs inspected us, uttered a few barks and lay down again. We crossed to the house through a host of chicken and ducks that clucked and quacked about us as if expecting grain from heaven. A trio of young lambs made a hesitant move forward and thought better of it.

At the garden gate there was a stiff broom, standard equipment at every house. We brushed our boots free of dirt, opened the gate and entered the garden. An unexpected feast of colour met my eyes. The Cape garden was an oasis of flowers in neat beds and borders surrounded by a driftwood fence to shelter the plants from the wind. Somebody was an ardent gardener.

Indoors, the living room seemed a sea of faces. Andreas introduced me to Stan and Muzzie. Stan was in his forties. Soft spoken with a lilting Somerset burr, he had a never ending fund of tales and anecdotes to recount. He obviously enjoyed the shepherd's outdoor life and had a healthy weathered tan. Muzzie was cheerful and practical. She was a very capable housewife used to catering for large numbers when the shepherds were billeted there at gathering times. When Muzzie 'got cracking' things moved whether she was making a dress, baking, milking cows or painting the roof of the house. It was Muzzie who nurtured the flower garden. Like so many of the island ladies she could turn her hand to pretty well anything.

13: Muzzie and Stan paint the roof.

Then there was Rab, the 'single' shepherd based at the Cape. Rab was lean-featured with jet-black hair and piercing eyes. In black sweater and black jeans he lacked only a Colt .45 to be the lone-star cowboy or hard-bitten rustler. When he was mounted with black thigh boots and hat pulled well down, the picture was complete. In reality Rab had a quiet disposition and never seemed harassed or out of sorts. He was well endowed with Falkland generosity and could always be relied upon if anyone needed a helping hand.

Next was Keith, Stan's second son, 14, who had just left school. He was fair-haired, slightly built and still with a schoolboy complexion. His heart was in horses and shepherding and he was very content with his lot. His younger brother and sister, Tony, nine, and, Jenny, seven, had the same fairness. They too enjoyed the open-air life of the Cape.

Yet Tony was about to leave home for three months. He had at last reached the top of the long waiting list for places at Darwin, the East Falkland boarding school. No more would his official education depend on the one week in eight average of the travelling teacher. Darwin School had a good name and parents were keen for their children to be there. In the morning Tony would ride into the settlement ready to fly to school. With him would go a large slab of butter for the Big House.

Mrs Cameron relied on Muzzie to keep the Big House in butter. Cape cows had good grazing. It was a large herd by island standards and roamed wide with the calving programme being left to the animals.

Pride of the herd was Pretty Cow. Pretty Cow had been noticed close to the boundary fence in Douglas Station Camp. If driven off she was back next day and in the end Stan and Rab decided she should be added to the Cape cows. Rab went rustling and Pretty Cow joined the herd. She calved, proved a good milker and added her quota to the Big House butter.

Each day began and ended with cows. The evening task of shutting the calves in the calf-house was essential so that next morning the cows would be at the paddock fence in mooing conversation with their offspring.

The milking shed was a good two hundred metres from the house across a small valley and in rain it seemed a long trudge. The first cow would be driven into the milking shed and her calf collected from the calf-pen for one or two sucks before being tied to a ringbolt so the cow could nuzzle it. The cow was then washed down and milked. Enough milk was left for the calf's needs and the pair were released into one of the paddocks where they stayed until the afternoon when the cows were parted from the calves and put out to graze. On fine days Jenny would help with a second cow outside but it was still a long job when 17 or 18 cows had to be looked after.

Most of the milk was put through a hand-operated separator for the cream, mainly destined to become butter for the Big House although there was always ample cream for the Cape table. Rich, fattening cream; glorious.

When milking was over, the separated milk was carried outside. In summer there was often a tub full and two cows, Kitty and Miranda Marie, who were very partial to milk, would sometimes come to blows over it. Miranda Marie, being polled, normally lost out to Kitty's horns.

14: Miranda Marie drinks her fill of separated milk.

The final task was to dismantle the separator and clean it with scalding water. That done, milking was over for the day.

Close to the milking shed was Stan's vegetable garden, again enclosed by high fencing. He had a good array of produce; salad, beans, greens, root crops and potatoes. The young root vegetables were enjoyed raw by the children almost like fruit. Apples and oranges were rare fare only coming to the islands at monthly intervals. Camp houses generally had to order fruit by the boxful through one of the Stanley shops. The order was sent to Montevideo via R.M.S. Darwin and the fruit would be sent on the return boat. Then it had to wait for transport to settlements when a Camp trip was made. Pears and bananas were almost exotic luxuries as they travelled badly and were as likely as not to be bordering on rottenness when they were unpacked.

Raspberries and gooseberries were a possibility given shelter and constant care. At KC, Murdo and Elizabeth had gradually established an area for soft fruit in their garden and had some wonderful crops.

In places there were wild strawberries. They ripened in January and February along with the deep red berries of diddle-dee. For most of the year diddle-dee was dull in even the brightest sun but when the abundant berries ripened they made an attractive splash of colour. The berries were fiddly to clean but made good jam or a clear jelly and were pleasant as a dessert.

If you got down on your hands and knees in the right sort of damp, moss-patched grass you could find the most delightful of all Falkland fruits, the tea-berry. They were white, blushed with pink and lay low among the ground level herbage. Fingers had to grope among stems for the biggest and juiciest and none was much bigger than a pea. Once you had acquired the taste you were hooked. You developed a flair for finding them but filling a tin instead of your mouth became a test of discipline. You had to concentrate on a vision of a bowl of tea-berries, sugar and cream or an open tea-berry tart fresh baked and topped with yet more cream.

Far easier to find, were the mushrooms. Sometimes, one of the Cape Dolphin valleys became carpeted with them, from tight buttons to ragged umbrellas. There was such a multitude that time could be wasted deciding which of them to pick. One morning, we decided to fill a bucket with the choicest mushrooms we could find. We were eyes down, intent on selecting the best, when a hail squall zipped over the valley side and battered us into our coats. The stones were fast, painful and numerous. Within a few minutes, the squall was across the valley and gone. Our carefully selected mushrooms floated limply in water and looked ruined. We grabbed the nearest and biggest around us to finish filling the bucket and made for the house, our feet squelching in our Wellingtons. Once back in the kitchen, Muzzie inspected our haul. She reckoned they were the cleanest mushrooms she had seen in ages. When a portion were fried and put on toast, we decided they were the tastiest as well.

The dominant summer meat was mutton. Mutton was tastily presented in many different ways but a change was always welcome. Upland-goose goslings provided the perfect substitute. If they were caught shortly before they learnt to fly there was plenty of meat on them but many people preferred them smaller. Each pair of geese kept their goslings to a restricted area. Once you had located a group you could keep your eye on them in order to take them at the optimum time. It was little different from stock rearing except that if you left your stock too long they flew away and you lost your meat.

One day Jenny took me in quest of goslings to the Cinnamon Valley where a stream ran through deep-green cinnamon grass. The geese were there and the next day's meat was caught. If there had been shops, perhaps the bloodiness of obtaining meat could have remained hidden.

In the islands, reality was the norm and the goslings were prepared for the oven.

15: The realities of food. Upland goslings fattening in the House Valley.

We continued down the valley to the shore. The tide was low and had left thick disks of red-brown jellyfish splodged about the sand. High by the dunes, an elephant seal lounged, huge, top heavy and cumbersome. It lay ignoring our inspection for some minutes before tiring of the intrusion and arching upwards to bellow its annoyance. Expressive tons of black blubber thumped down onto the sands and we decided to go. The elephant seal was not as clumsy as it looked.

The goslings became a very satisfying supper served with fresh vegetables from the garden and followed by a large helping of tea-berry tart and cream.

A quiet evening followed; Muzzie relaxing in the rocking-chair with her sewing, Stan on the settee selecting strips of neatly torn material for the half-finished rug across his knees, the sound of the waves still sighing on the sands and the calves mad-racing round their paddock in the last of the light. Cape Dolphin at peace.

16: Cape Dolphin at peace.

RICKETY IN PART

Cape Dolphin being the northernmost house to visit, it was time to return to San Carlos. Ray and Mary, Patrick's parents, were taking their first turn in lodging the teacher.

Ray's house was just outside the Big House garden, convenient for his work as gardener and close enough to be wired for electricity from Mr Bonner's generator. It was switched on each evening from dusk until ten which guaranteed power for the lights and radio. Apart from the generating times, almost the only outside noise was when somebody reached the white shell path leading to the front door. Ray and Mary always knew when a visitor was approaching.

When the fortnight's school session finished, Gerald acted as guide to Sussex, the next house on the itinerary. Sussex was the home of Frank and Jean with their daughter, Ellen, and three youngest boys, Tubby, Sydney and Robin. The two oldest sons, David and Lars, worked at the settlement and lived there in the cookhouse.

The weather was perfect and our coats could stay strapped behind the saddles. George by now had left the islands and was somewhere at sea on his way home to England. I had inherited his regulation issue riding gear; a large wooden saddle, stirrups set on rusty-buckled straps at a length suitable for George's long legs, a rather meagre cojinillo which little more than covered the saddle and a well worn pair of maletas. We tried to alter the stirrup length but the rust beat us and we decided not to bother.

The horse was named Mischief, a ten-year-old light chestnut. Mischief had not been worked much recently and was consequently rather fat. When I mounted him it was like being astride a barrel with my legs spread so wide that my feet finished short of the stirrups.

We set off across the green by the cookhouse, down and up the dip by the jetty, past the shearing shed and through the next gully by which time I very much wanted to bother to alter the stirrups. We stopped at the gate to adjust them.

Thirty minutes later we were still there but had at last managed to prise each buckle open, clean the worst of the rust off and set the stirrups at a better length. We continued across Burnt Camp Paddock which was firm and level. To our left were the hills and to our right was the creek.

It was becoming an enjoyable ride. I set the pace at a fast amble and Gerald did his best to keep back with me. For twenty minutes or so the enjoyment continued. Then I became aware that the gear had worked loose and my balance was not quite right. It was nothing much, just a slight tilt to my left with the saddle a bit off centre.

I pushed my left foot against the stirrup to regain a proper balance. The saddle moved further round, taking me with it. The saddle's speed accelerated. I clawed despairingly at the horse's neck, had a fleeting upside-down sensation and hit Burnt Camp hard and true in time to watch Mischief's surprised jump as the gear settled under his ample belly.

I felt the complete idiot and scrambled to my feet. Mischief stood by patiently. We put the gear to rights and set off again. At first all was well but then the feeling of unease began again. I was slipping. Or was it just imagination? It was hard to be sure because Mischief had broken into a gentle trot which perforce made me unstable.

Uncertain of my balance, I decided to check the gear. I pulled on the reins. Mischief stopped with a slight jolt and the saddle slipped sideways again. I hit Burnt Camp with exactly the same part of me as before, only harder, while the gear once more settled beneath Mischief's belly.

Once more we sorted the gear out and this time we pulled the cincha tighter. Full of misgivings I remounted. I suppose it was fortunate I had been landing on my hip and not my backside for there was still plenty of ride ahead of us. Mischief settled into an easy trot and I bumped up and down trying to put the next fall out of my mind.

Happily, there were no more falls that day. We negotiated Head of the Bay Brook, slowly crossed Sussex Mountain and arrived at the house. The ride had been time consuming but the sun was still high in the sky and at least the horses had not been pushed too fast.

The situation was pleasant; the creek in front and a view one way to Mount Usborne and the other way to the mountains of West Falkland.

The house was 98 years old, rickety in parts but generally sound and strong. It had yellow painted weather boarding, sash windows of the old fashioned small-paned kind, a near vertical stairway to the upper rooms, a low dark sitting-room and a long kitchen.

The kitchen held Jean's pride and joy; a glorious, double ovened, Victorian range with a small water tank at the end ensuring constant hot water. Ellen had the task of ensuring the water tank was topped up every time any was used. It was Ellen who kept the stove spotlessly shiny black and Tubby who made sure the peat box was full of neatly chopped sods to keep the fire at an even heat.

17: The house beside the creek at Sussex.

Frank had looked after Sussex for several years. He was an experienced shepherd who had moved around Camp on both East and West Falkland. Jean was used to life in an outside shepherd's house but she did miss the company of neighbours. As a result, the R/T messages assumed great importance for her and remained 'on' as she worked about the house. She was an excellent cook, particularly adept at making drop-scones. They were wafer thin and when hot and finely spread with syrup they melted in your mouth and left it watering for more.

Jean was also very fond of playing whist but was unable to attend many of the settlement drives. With the extra person making a game possible for her, we would sit until the small hours playing hand after hand, fortified by coffee and whatever sort of cakes she had baked that day.

Breakfast was not until nine and not until breakfast was finished in leisurely style did the boys adjourn to the sitting-room for school. Once there, they worked hard enough at a very basic curriculum but with only two weeks' schooling in every sixteen it had to be that way. At four o'clock, lessons ended. Within minutes the boys were out of school-clothes, into comfy gear and out of the house to make the most of the remaining daylight.

It was April, early autumn, but without the colour of a British autumn. Evenings had drawn in and it was dark by six. Supper was eaten by Tilley lamp light. The radio was tuned to the Falkland Islands Broadcasting Station for the evening transmission. It began with announcements, messages and the next day's flight schedule. At seven o'clock was the B.B.C. World News followed by a mix of B.B.C. and local programmes.

Most popular of the local programmes were the quizzes between Town and Camp teams, the Stanley plays and 'Friday Hour' record requests. Every settlement had its particular song either to recall a local incident or with someone to fit the lyrics. At KC, it was Tom Smith; the Mr Smith who had triggered the confusion on the R/Ts over George's lost books. As soon as the plaintive country and western, "Hang down your head, Tom Dooley", hit the Falkland airwaves, KC had their man. Tom Smith became Tom Dooley for ever more. "Hang down your head and cry," demanded the song, although anyone more cheerful than Tom would be hard to imagine. The out and out favourite among the men was "The Pub With No

Beer", a lilting Australian song engendering awful visions of a weekend with no liquor ration. There, the tears could easily have rolled.

Each evening, when transmissions ended for the night and the National Anthem was being played, the link with Britain seemed renewed. "God Save Our Queen" was a reassuring ending to the day.

The start of the day had become less dependable. The weather was turning cold. Frost covered the ground and coated the windows with a delicate tracery that seemed more firmly outlined each morning. Getting up became a chore. Between the bed and the door was another piece of Sussex Victoriana, a marbled wash-stand complete with ewer and basin. Each day Ellen carried water from the well, refilled the ewer and stood it beside the basin. Each morning I had sooner or later to get out of bed and pay homage to it.

I made great efforts to imagine I enjoyed washing in cold water and that it was actually exhilarating, but the day I poured cat-ice into the basin I gave up pretending and swore. It was inwardly warming and helped no end. After washing, I poured a bit more water into the basin for effect and made for the glorious Victorian range where there would be a pot of tea, well stewed by the time I got there but still hot and comforting.

18: Sussex horses grazing. The background is Mount Usborne.

On the eighth, we woke to see snow across the hills of West Falkland and on Mount Usborne. The next morning we awoke to a blizzard. Pictures of Antarctic wastes sprang to mind but when two men arrived from the settlement after breakfast to carry out T.B. tests on the cattle, the blizzard had to be down graded to heavy snow.

Rounding up the cattle from the hills, herding them to the House Paddock and carrying out the tests took all week. Each animal was lassoed ready to be brought close to a post in the corner of the corral. Some accepted reluctantly. Others reacted violently, bellowing, laying back on their haunches and obliging three men to haul on the rope and Frank's dogs to snap at the cow's heels before the animal could be secured. The vet then used calipers to measure the thickness of the hide on the neck and prepared his syringe. When the needle went in, the cows objected anew, kicking and butting at everything in sight. T.B. testing provided plenty of entertainment.

When the tests were finally concluded and the results analysed, the vet was able to declare a clean bill of health. We drank the milk with an easier mind.

The milking parlour was the post in the corner of the corral and pasteurization simply could not happen. Ellen and Tubby did the milking. When the weather was fine, they milked in the dry and when there was rain or snow they milked in that and just went quicker. Thus the worse the weather the greater proportion of milk going to the calf, a system which catered for both milker and animal.

Sydney and Robin helped with the meat supply by providing the occasional upland goose hunted with bolas. The boys' bolas were Y shaped lengths of cord with equal weighted cow vertebrae on the leading cords and a lighter one on the tail.

The boys gave me a few lessons aiming at a peat-bucket on the green. I could manage twirling the bolas above my head but letting go at the right moment seemed beyond me. Nevertheless, I was invited on one of their missions.

Off we went to procure the evening meal. We sighted some geese and Sydney manoeuvred us upwind of them so that their take-off flight would start towards us.

When the geese sensed danger, they began a tell tale head-nodding.

Sydney's strict instruction was to freeze at the signal until the birds settled down again.

As soon as the geese's accelerated nodding indicated imminent take-off, we had to whirl our bolas above our heads, choose a target, aim in front of it and judge the right time to let fly.

The time came. Away whizzed the bolas, leading edges spread wide, straight as an arrow above, below or between birds which seemed far more likely to catch us with a backside squirt as they flew past than we ever were to catch them. The following quarter of an hour or so was spent hunting bolas.

The sequence was consistent throughout the afternoon; sight, stalk, throw and search, varying only in the search interval. Two of us may have weakened a little but Sydney was determined and persevered until he had caught three geese. These he plucked and gutted ready for cooking. They proved tasty birds.

The boys took me on several more expeditions but I was still miles wide of my first bird when the time came to leave Sussex and ride to the final house on my beat, Wreck Point.

Wreck Point

Wreck Point was only 90 minutes ride away from Sussex but moving-weekend coincided with a whist drive and dance at Port San Carlos. Everyone at San Carlos had been invited and most people intended to go, which would leave JB settlement pretty well empty, an even quieter weekend than usual for the manager and his wife.

The KC farm boat, Redwing, came round to collect the visitors. Redwing was about eight metres in length and comfortingly broad with a rather dumpy mast and a white sail loosely bound about the boom. Motive power was a sturdy engine housed in the cabin, the sail an emergency stand-by. The 15 passengers constituted a crowd and most had to go down in the hold forward of the mast.

Redwing chugged competently down the creek, around Hospital Point and along to KC where passengers were thankful to disembark. The unventilated, lightless hold had no comforts, not even proper seating.

Visitors dispersed to the various houses where they were to have lodgings.

At 8 o'clock the whist drive began in the cookhouse dining-room. The glow from the fire, its peaty perfume and whist played in close-set fours around a pair of wooden trestle tables, ensured conviviality during play and virtual hilarity sorting places at each change of partners.

When whist finished, the tables were cleared back to reveal the dance floor, smooth, shiny, specially cleaned linoleum good enough for everyone.

Falkland dances catered for everyone; from the heavy heeled to the nimble footed. The Valeta Waltz required only brief moments of proper waltzing amid a series of to and fro walking steps; a really

19: Andreas provides the dance music, Gerald and Sydney look on.

satisfying dance for anyone who could not tell a waltz from a quickstep. Where necessary, the lady dancing the one, two, three, hop of the polka, would cheerfully chant the step to help her partner forward.

A master of ceremonies made sure the dance mix kept people happy. If he called a fox-trot, the decent dancers had the floor to themselves while non dancers sat and jiggled to the rhythm. A simpler dance would follow giving everybody the chance to take part and set the floor bouncing to a Gay Gordons or Palais Glide.

The M.C. kept the dance going until evening became three o'clock morning, when he called the last waltz. It was time for sleep on bed, sofa, chair or floor.

People awoke to find mist through the valley. The creek was like a millpond. San Carlos visitors were rounded up from the houses and by noon Redwing was away, round Hospital Point again and heading for the Ajax Bay Freezer jetty.

There the Wreck Point party stepped ashore, to the surprise of the old caretaker. Half-an-hour later they were home and John's wife had the fire going and a kettle on for coffee.

Wreck Point house lay close against the lower slopes of Campito Hill which rose 300 metres to a cragged summit. When, on a sunny winter's afternoon, Wreck Point became trapped in early shadows, a scramble up Campito would be rewarded by marvellous sunsets across the Falkland Sound. The rocky summit was home to a pair of hawks, wary but jealous of their space, cruising the crags for mice and small birds and 'keeowing' a protest against human intrusion until evening gloom forced a descent to supper.

The next weekend a grand dance was being held at Darwin settlement where the draw was to be made for one of the big Falkland sweepstakes. It was a popular gamble with 36000 tickets sold among the islanders. First prize was £500, equal to my annual salary, with over 100 smaller prizes. Somebody was going to feel rich.

Several San Carlos people were riding over to Darwin and John guided me on Mischief to Head of the Bay to join them. The ground was snow covered but from Sussex Mountain there was a clear tractor track to follow down to the creek.

The tide was low and we were able to splash our way across saving several miles ride round the top of the creek. The way was now more or less level and in a couple of hours we had reached Darwin.

Sleep for several of us that night would be in Goose Green cookhouse a mile or so further on. We were taken there by Land Rover. The cook showed us to our rooms. We changed into dance clothes and returned to Darwin.

The evening's dancing began at eight and the hall was soon full. Music was provided by anyone able to play the piano-accordion or violin. At first, only the competent dancers took the floor but gradually the less lithesome joined. The atmosphere brightened when a Gay Gordons gave the chance for the men to show their paces. When the M.C. announced a Palais Glide, everyone could have a go. The accordionist struck up, "There was I waiting at the church", and people linked arms in fives or sixes across the floor making a

20: Heather and Gyd dance a Gay Gordons. Heather, Stan and Muzzie's older daughter, was a wonderfully vivacious, generous person greatly missed by everyone.

perfectly safe support for anyone wanting a dance but whose feet were a bit whisky-befused for the waltzes and quicksteps.

With a Palais Glide under their belts, the dancers were really in the mood and the musicians gave them good value. Waltz, quickstep, Highland Schottische for the experts and back to the Palais Glide; the dances went on. When one musician tired or ran out of tunes, another took over and the master of ceremonies saw to it that a fair number of slower dances were played to help the ladies. They were far outnumbered by the men yet they kept on their feet for dance after dance, only declining when utterly exhausted. One or two of the men on the other hand had been off their feet before the dance began. They had enjoyed their bottle to the full, or empty, and would not remember much of the evening at all.

The dances were interspersed with draws for the sweepstake. Sets of numbered ping-pong balls tumbled in true lottery fashion and when the revolving drum came to rest, five numbers recorded a lucky winner.

When the drums rolled for the top prize, every person in the hall was silent. The rattle of tumbling ping-pong balls stopped; the die was cast. A sweepstake organiser read out the winning number but no whoop of delight broke the silence. No dancer held the lucky ticket.

The list of ticket holders was referred to and the winner named. It was Rab from Cape Dolphin. Not until the radio broadcast the dance report next evening, would he hear of his win.

The MC called another Palais Glide. People crowded the floor. There was still the dance to enjoy.

At five o'clock the last waltz was played and people dispersed for a few hours' sleep.

It was deep afternoon before we set off home and dusk had enshrouded the track by the time the San Carlos people said "Cheerio" at Head of the Bay. John had had the forethought to say that I should ring from there and he would ride out to guide me to Wreck Point.

Head of the Bay house was in darkness. I hitched Mischief to a post and looked for the front door. No one answered my knock but the place was not locked and I decided to go inside. I groped for the phone, found it in a corner of the room and gave the five rings for Wreck Point. No answer. I tried twice more and realized the phone was dead. There would be no guide.

None too cheerful, I remounted Mischief. He set off willingly enough and was soon at an inlet of the creek. The tide was low but crossing unfamiliar water in the dark was not exactly enjoyable. Thankfully Mischief took his time and safely reached firm ground again. He trotted on.

Within minutes the ground had softened. The trot became a walk and the darkness turned colder. Suddenly Mischief whinnied. There were answering whinnies, the noise of hoofs squelching in soft ground and we were surrounded by riderless horses jostling each other and nosing close against us. One brushed past my right leg, another pressed against my left. We could not move. Their nostrils snorted curiosity and I was decidedly uncomfortable.

In another flurry of squelching hoofs they were gone. We were more alone than ever in an eerie silence with the ground so soft it seemed a swamp. I hurriedly dismounted and began leading Mischief left towards higher ground. My feet sank in mud or I stumbled over tussocks and progress was painfully slow. Then my foot trod on nothing. I hurtled headlong down a bank and Mischief balanced perilously on the brink. I scrambled back up to him. How many more edges to the world were there?

Progress slowed even more and stopped. A strand of wire barred my way, I had walked into a fence. It was good news. A fence must sooner or later have a gate and a chance to find the track again. To follow the fence up Campito Hill would be daft. I turned right. The gate materialised.

Once through the gate I decided to let Mischief try for the track again. I mounted and ahead of me was a faint star, so low on the horizon it had to be man made. Glory of glories.

Mischief trotted on and I guided for the star. There were streams, and bog, and rock and frozen snow but the star glowed brighter. At last it became a hazy window. The window sharpened and around it Wreck Point formed.

I was home, thanks to John's Tilley lighthouse in the bedroom window. Bed was especially good that night.

DIGGING OUT

From Wreck Point I returned to the settlement for a week's leave. Three of us had booked to fly to Stanley to collect an ex-U.S. Army jeep that had arrived from England on A.E.S, the wool-boat. Big John, the farm mechanic, was the new owner and Terry, a Hampshire man out there on a five year contract, was to drive it back to San Carlos. I was hitching a lift; my first experience of Falkland Island cross-country driving.

A second jeep had been bought by Pat, a young Darwin shepherd. This was important because it meant we could travel as a pair, a wise precaution in Camp driving.

"Bogging" in soft ground was the bane of the Camp driver and plenty of advice was offered, "Don't travel in winter if it's not essential. If you have to travel, don't drive." Others reflected that in summer you bogged so often you spent more time in mud holes than in actual driving; whereas, in winter you bogged only once and spent the rest of the time digging yourself out.

It was June, mid-winter. Certainly the drivers were well prepared for trouble having planks, shovels, ropes and iron stakes for varied contingences. Pat was to lead as he knew the Camp better and Terry was to follow at a safe distance so that both jeeps would not finish in the same hole at the same time.

Big John spent a couple of days checking the jeep. It proved in good order except that it needed a tow to make it start, and the lights did not work.

Early next day we were on our way. It was cold and, according to the forecast, getting colder. For the first seven miles beyond Stanley where the track was rough and pot-holed the jeep bounced around a fair deal. From then on the bouncing ceased for the road was as wide as the horizon and the surface pure grassland.

Camp driving required a completely different technique from driving on roads. The drivers had to be ready to respond to what the vehicle was doing almost as much as to dictate what should be happening. Pat led the way, avoiding the softest spots, and finding fordable places at the streams.

We were in a fold of the hills when the inevitable happened. Terry's wheels lost grip, dug into the ground and the jeep was bogged. The ground was too soft for Pat to risk stopping and he drove in a wide circle waiting for us. Fortunately we were not in deep and with Big John and myself pushing while Terry carefully let in the clutch the jeep was soon moving again.

As if on cue, Pat buried his front axle in a narrow ditch. Terry promptly stopped. Spades and planking were produced and Big John dug the soil away so that the planks could be pushed beneath Pat's wheels. The tow rope was fastened, Pat climbed aboard his jeep and Big John and I went round to push. Terry inched back taking in the slack. The rope held, the planks sank in as the weight of the jeep went on them and Pat was back on level ground. Quickly the rope was unhitched, planks were recovered and stowed with the spades, we climbed back aboard and the vehicles moved off again, Terry now keeping a clear 30 metres behind in case of similar ditches.

Within five minutes, Pat was down again, this time by the back wheels. Digging recommenced while Terry manoeuvred his vehicle for the tow. Pat's wheels were in really deep and much more soil had to be moved. It was sweaty work and as each spade-full was thrown out an almost equal amount of mud oozed back into the hole, sweaty and frustrating.

Then, as one, everybody stopped. Something was missing, the noise of Terry's jeep. Great! One in the ditch and the other stalled and a doubtful starter – 6 to 4 against by the look on Terry's face. Spades were dropped and it was all hands to Terry's jeep.

Pushing a jeep on tarmac may be peanuts; on soft peat it is different. But shove it had to be, and was, to a slight decline where the jeep began rolling a little more easily. With Terry jiggling the controls there came a sudden surge of life. The jeep was back in action. We piled aboard and drove over to finish digging out Pat's vehicle.

Four more times a jeep bogged and four more times we had to resort to planks, spades, tow ropes and sweat before that particular group of hills was crossed.

We came down to sea-level on the beach at Bluff Cove and hugged the coast line towards Fitzroy. Speed increased a bit but it did not seem to account for anything because the more corners we turned the more there were ahead of us and the greater the expanse of frozen beach and ice-edged sea.

There too the first snow squall hit us and progress slowed again. Snow shrouded everything. Sea and beach disappeared. The jeep jolted slowly on. The canvas hood was good but not weather proof. Snowflakes clustered round the crannies. They crept through the cracks, drifted around and settled silently to melt and trickle coldly down the neck until clothing absorbed them.

Gradually the squall eased. When it was past and the scenery returned, the white beach looked colder than ever. Wheel tracks trailed back around a headland. Another bay was followed by another and at last we climbed onto the Fitzroy track to bump our way to the settlement where we had smoko and thawed out.

Pat and Big John checked the vehicles and we set off once more hoping to reach Darwin about seven as there was a clear track. Good progress was made until dusk when things became more difficult. Because of the lack of lights on his jeep, Terry had to follow Pat's tail light. This was alright until a gully was reached and Pat's light disappeared. Terry had to gauge the right line to take until he could see the lights again. Darwin would not be reached by seven.

It was difficult for Pat to judge the following jeep's speed. At one gully he was actually up the far bank before Terry began the descent. There was obviously a bend in the track because Pat had come out at a different angle from going in. Terry nosed down, somehow located the bend at the bottom and began following it. Part way round, there was a violent lurch and the jeep toppled sideways at a crazy angle. I was on my back, covered by luggage. One hand was in flowing water numbingly cold. I thrust my hand in my pocket and lay wondering vaguely where my hat was.

"You O.K.?" boomed a voice. I came to with a jerk.

"Yes." I pushed the luggage away, found my hat was across my face, rummaged for my ruck-sack and climbed out. The others were inspecting the jeep. Both offside wheels were deep in a ditch. It would certainly be sitting there that night.

We walked out of the gully and saw Pat some distance off no doubt wondering what the delay was. There was no point going back to assess the damage so Pat had three passengers. His jeep was minus the canvas hood and the squalls were pretty continuous but at least we were getting where we wanted until we arrived at a shepherd's house and Pat realised we were heading off on the wrong track.

"Mount Pleasant Shanty," he informed us. He made an abrupt about turn and soon regained the way. The track was well worn now and the ice-filmed puddles were more akin to water-holes. The jeep splashed into an extra deep one, there was a gurgle and we stopped in mid-water. A rapid inspection showed the water to be coincidental; the trouble was a lamentable lack of petrol.

We set off on the eight miles walk to Darwin. The snow reflected what little light there was and our eyes soon adjusted to it. Two and a half hours later we arrived at Pat's house and awaiting us was a huge three course meal. Bliss.

The next day was a lazy one for Big John and myself as there was no room on the salvage party's tractor. That evening both jeeps arrived none the worse for wear.

On Tuesday morning we set out on the last stage of the journey to Sussex and San Carlos. As there was a well used track all the way, we had no worries about being the only vehicle. Sussex was reached in good time with only two delays for slight engine trouble. We had dinner there and commenced the final leg. Half way up Sussex Mountain the jeep gave up the struggle with a burnt out clutch. We were walking again.

The walk to San Carlos seemed no distance at all but JB was not my destination. I had to collect my gear and continue to KC. At the settlement they provided me with a horse, the Navvy Sino. The Navvy Sino had the reputation of being the most uncomfortable horse for miles around but it was reliable. It could also be trusted to find its way back to the settlement fence from KC point, which meant nobody need accompany me to look after the horse.

A rough ride was far better than being on foot. I had an added mission too. There was a considerable bundle of packages to go across for Grandad Dickson, Old John, who was staying at Bill and Clara's where he had just celebrated his 76th birthday.

Being postman for Old John made me feel good. The Navvy Sino's shuffling gait was hardly noticeable. At KC point, I spent three quarters of an hour yelling for a boat and lighting a diddle-dee fire to attract attention. Time did not matter. I had enjoyed an eventful jeep drive from Stanley and would soon have the pleasure of delivering Old John's mail.

"Go Seek!"

Old John had arrived by plane from one of the outer island farms the previous week. The Land Rover had collected him from the jetty and taken him up to Clara's in fine style. Old John was tough and wiry, spry in spirit and in action too as far as his rheumatics allowed him but a lifetime of shepherding and riding rebel horses had left its mark and now he needed a stick to steady his legs. In his younger days he had reckoned nothing of riding the width of West Falkland to get astride a horse that had some challenge in it. Now his greatest pleasure was his pipe.

Just now Old John's pipe was going well and he was as content as could be expected on an evening when the wind shook the house and found every chink and draughtway. The Rayburn fire-door was open and Old John sat beside it soaking up the warmth. Not that he sat all day taking his ease. He still set himself a work programme and helped about the house. After supper that evening he had been giving a hand to clear the dishes when he slipped on the kitchen step. Bill had helped him to his feet and Old John had grumbled at his own "silly clumsiness", glad only that he had not broken Clara's cups. He declared he had not hurt himself but it had shaken him up a bit so he was sitting by the fire 'taking things quiet'. On the hot-plate the kettle grumbled in low key, too much heat was going through the open door. Old John puffed his pipe and thought.

Clara sat at the table addressing a final envelope ready for the next day's plane. It was the usual last-minute rush to complete letters for the outgoing mail from the islands. Somehow correspondence always got pushed to one side until the final posting announcement on the radio made letter writing a priority. Bill was in the sitting-room panelling the walls. He hoped to have them finished and the room repainted in time for the dog trials being held at KC that weekend.

The dog trials were for the North Camp area. The islands were split into a number of areas and the three best dogs from each would be entered in the Stanley trials to decide the champion of champions. Port San Carlos was hosting the north trials and using the occasion for a 'two-nighter' dance to mark the opening of the new hall that was nearing completion. No longer would the cookhouse double as a community centre.

The building comprised a dance-hall, kitchen and school room. The old Nissen hut school could rust to nothing. Building had begun as soon as the season's shearing had ended and work had progressed steadily. Electricity was to be provided by a small petrol-driven generator. A large peat-fired stove in the kitchen would power central heating. The frame and walling had gone up in quick time but difficulties kept arising with the plumbing and wiring so that it seemed doubtful whether the interior decorating could be completed in time for the trials.

The ladies too were working against time. Every house would be inundated with visitors, and larders had to be filled in readiness. Each day became a baking day – cakes, buns, biscuits and finally bread. The flour was from a huge 50 kg sack, each portion carefully sieved for purity, and the sugar from a 25 kg sack. Eggs were from the household's own hens. Everything had to be baked in the Rayburn oven and the husband's task was to chop plenty of peat to the size most efficient for keeping the oven at an even heat. The flour and sugar in the sacks lessened noticeably as the stack of full tins increased in the larder.

By Friday, plumbing and baking had both somehow been completed. Hall and housewives were ready.

In the afternoon the first of the visitors arrived, riders from Douglas Station and Teal Inlet. Across the creek a group of walkers could be seen, tiny dots descending the mountain. It would be some time before they arrived on the point opposite the settlement and if the wind got up much more there would be difficulties in rowing them across. Already, at midday, Mr Cameron had made a 'blind' R/T call informing San Carlos that the wind was too high for Redwing to collect them. Somebody at JB had obviously been tuned to 4.5

9: R.M.S. Darwin at Port San Carlos unloading horses from Chile.

10: The social side of the ship's visit. Clara with Fraser, Leona and Arina visit friends aboard the Darwin. The fuel is for the Port San Carlos tractors.

11: John and Billy Gull ride to San Carlos with the cattle. One will become beef.

12: The bullock that broke Keith's lasso. Gyd surveys the beef he and the navvy gang
helped convert the day the pickaxes met too much Cape Dolphin rock.

13: Shearing at Port San Carlos. Tom Dooley takes his turn as wool boy.
Fred grades the quality of the fleeces.

14: Driving sheep through diddle-dee in Smylies Village heading towards Cape Dolphin.
Captain Smylie was a semi-piratical seal hunter of the nineteenth century.

15: San Carlos railway. Bales being taken on the trolley to the end of the jetty ready for the wool ship. One trip, the trolley ran out of control and jettisoned bales into the creek.

16: The wool ship A.E.S. at San Carlos. Bales are being winched aboard from the scows, the flat bottomed barges used in shallow waters around the settlements.

megs or there would not be the walkers on the mountain.

Two of the cookhouse men went to the jetty and commenced lowering the boat. For once, people on the point would not have to shout and gesticulate hoping to attract attention, not that shouting in that wind would have had any effect.

In the settlement, people were making their way to the new hall for a film. The central heating was proving adequate and the new chairs, stackable steel-framed with stretched canvas, were comfortable. Tom, the handyman, set the first reel in motion and everybody settled to watch *The Cruel Sea*, a trifle ironic for San Carlos people still descending the mountain.

Visitors continued to arrive and eventually they outnumbered the KC people. The evening's dancing followed the usual pattern with the usual energy and lasted until three o'clock. It allowed just enough sleep for the morning's dog trials.

By nine o'clock, people were assembling beyond the shearing shed. The trial was for the shepherd to send his dog away to collect five sheep released from a pen higher on the hillside and for the dog to bring the sheep down the hill, around set obstacles and into a second pen. Each entry was allowed fifteen minutes, at which time a bell would sound. Points were awarded for the gather, the drive and the penning. There were twelve dogs entered, three of them owned by a shepherd from Teal Inlet.

Up on the hill behind the releasing pen the ground dipped away. If the sheep took it into their heads to move off in that direction they were out of sight before the shepherd could get his dog up to them. It happened to the second man. He whistled his dog on as it disappeared beyond the pen. There came moments of suspense, entertaining for spectators but excruciating for the shepherd whose dog was on show, would it or would it not return with the sheep?

The shepherd waited, whistled and waited. A sheep came partially into view and went again. At last three came over followed by the dog but of the other two there was no sign. When the bell sounded, the dog was still valiantly trying to reunite the sheep.

One or two dogs did not find the sheep at all and reappeared rather bewildered to be upbraided by their masters. Another dog set off at high speed and could be heard barking industriously over the ridge where the odd bleat suggested he'd located the sheep but, whistle as the shepherd may, neither dog nor sheep came back. At the end of his time the shepherd marched up the hill, sighted the animals and whistled anew. The dog responded and brought the sheep down in fine style to be applauded by the spectators keen to do something to warm their hands on a chilly June morning.

David, the shepherd from Teal Inlet, was having better luck. The first of his dogs located the sheep at once, moved them slowly down the hill, negotiated the obstacles and worked towards the pen. David quietly pulled the gate wide, commanded his dog and the sheep were edged towards the pen and safely enclosed. He swung the gate to with quiet satisfaction. The applause was well earned. David was again successful with his second dog and his third was working the sheep towards the pen when the bell sounded.

Bill had entered Glen, one of his most reliable dogs, but Glen got off to a bad start. Once each set of sheep was used they were put into the next paddock where they stayed huddled in a bottom corner. Glen set off straight for those sheep. Bill recalled him and set him off up the hill but precious minutes had been lost. Glen disappeared beyond the releasing pen. Bill whistled commands and Glen reappeared over the brow with the five sheep neatly bunched. He brought them down, controlled them through the obstacles and held them in front of the pen. Bill opened the gate and called Glen on. The sheep moved quietly inwards as if drawn by a magnet. At which moment the bell clanged 'Time', and that was that; so near and yet so far.

At the end of the morning the judges compared notes and announced the result; first David from Teal Inlet, second David again, third Bill with Glen. Shepherds, dogs and spectators went to dinner leaving the sheep the peace of the hillside.

During the afternoon there was an auction in the shearing shed. Furniture, books and household items came under the hammer and raised a good sum for the Stanley Red Cross Ambulance Fund.

The auction was followed by the children's party in the hall organised by the cookhouse men. They had made a giant slide, a see-saw and a pillow-fight 'horse' where the children sat astride a pole and batted away at each other with great gusto. A couple of the men became panto-mothers for an Aunt Sally and spent their time failing to dodge wet sponges. It was all high glee for the children.

21: Stuart in charge of the see-saw and slide at the children's party.

When the party finished, the hall was cleared ready for the second night's dancing. It kept a lively pace through to the small hours of morning when it was deemed enough was enough.

By Sunday evening all of the visitors had returned home, KC was peaceful and Old John was able to relax by the fire and enjoy a quiet pipe again.

"Did She Bolt With You?"

Douglas Station had been added to my teaching circuit. The Saturday following the dog trials, it was time to move there with Rab as my guide. After dinner we set off.

The way took us over the shoulder of Cerro Montevideo, KC's highest ground, from where we looked across a series of valleys towards Douglas Station with Mount Usborne and No Man's Land far away to our right. From Cerro Montevideo there was a reasonably marked track to an outside shepherd's house with a name that hinted of royal connections, Newhouse of Glamis. However inspiring the house might once have been, it was now in sore need of a coat of paint. The position did not help either, stuck in the middle of nowhere with nothing particular around it except a series of streams filled to the brim with winter water.

We gave the horses a breather at Newhouse of Glamis and looked for Oscar, the shepherd there. As he was not in, we took advantage of his unfailing hospitality to put the kettle across the stove for a cup of tea. We phoned Douglas Station to let them know we were on the way but none of our rings carried anywhere, the line was dead.

We brewed the tea, spent a lazy half hour drinking it, washed the mugs, filled Oscar's peat bin by way of a thank you, made up the fire and set off again.

A little later we met Oscar on the track. He had been out tracing a break in the telephone line and had just succeeded in mending it. He promised to ring Douglas for us.

By supper time we were at the settlement and I had been delivered to Marj and Owen whose two boys, Terence and Ian, would constitute half the class. Six year old, Jane, younger daughter of the head shepherd, would be the only girl. Jane, who had an older brother and sister away at Darwin Boarding School, was well used to standing up for herself. Brian, just beginning school, completed the class.

Douglas Station settlement lay beside a narrow unnavigable creek which seemed to have wandered off pointlessly from Salvador Waters, the large almost land-locked tidal stretch that included Salvador, Teal Inlet, Rincon Grande and outside houses belonging to several other farms.

Douglas was renowned for one great weakness, a five mile journey to reach the Moro, the nearest water suitable for the Beavers. When Douglas was on the flights, close co-operation with Stanley Control was essential to ensure the settlement Land-Rover was on time for ferrying passengers to or from the Moro.

Christine and Charles, with whom I had stayed when I was first at San Carlos, had recently moved to Douglas. Their complete furniture had been piled on open trailers and hauled over the hills by tractor. Knowing them helped make the place feel an integral part of the circuit.

The first week there proved cold, very cold. The days were short and the long July nights brought sharp frosts.

Saturday morning dawned frosty as ever but with red taints of shepherd's warning in the sky. I had arranged to ride across to KC with homework for Clara's girls that I should have set instead of enjoying the 'two-nighter'. Jane's father had said I could borrow Princess for the trip, a tame, trustworthy mount although she had a tendency to start quickly. As long as I turned her towards the fence when remounting at gates she would give me a good ride. The way was clear enough via Newhouse of Glamis. Provided I left early enough to allow time for going off course occasionally, I would not need a guide.

After breakfast I went out to the green to catch Princess. She seemed an even keener starter than predicted. The green was empty. Possibly she had wandered off to the wool-shed at the far end of the settlement to find shelter.

I clumped off along the frost-hard ground in my cumbersome leather riding-boots, past Christine's house where two rows of washing were already hanging on the lines, past Marj and Owen's new house, round by the head shepherd's and across the wooden bridge to the pens at the shearing shed. There was still no sign of Princess but there was an open gate at the far end. If Princess had found her way through the twists and turns of the pens she could be out in the paddock.

It was a large paddock and sure enough at the far end stood Princess rubbing noses with a friend across the fence. She allowed herself to be caught without trouble and led back across the green to the stable. I geared her and hitched her to a rail while I went in for the books and a hot drink. Squalls could be seen passing between Douglas and the mountains. The red taints of shepherd's warning were a reality.

After a warming coffee, I said "Cheerio" and went outside to discover that Princess had disappeared again. So much for the securing hitch. There was only one place she could be, and she was. I found her in the nearby shed eating oats from the store of winter feed. I led her out just as Ron, the cowman, was returning from the cows, his two dogs at his heel.

With another "Cheerio", I mounted. One of the dogs barked as if in reply and away went the horse, hell for leather, a dashing Princess with a teacher clasping her neck.

Full thundering gallop down the green by Charles' peat shed, past the back of his house, through Christine's washing flapping ahead, above and behind us; a blur of Owen's new house, a swerving left by the head shepherd's, clatter on the wooden bridge and full steam into the sheep-pens. There Princess slithered to a halt unable to negotiate the tight turns. She stood snorting and blowing against a fence. I sat regaining my composure, wondering whether to cancel the trip or continue. The appearance of Ian and Jane decided things.

"Did she bolt with you?"

"Did you want to come this way?"

"Not exactly. She decided to take off with me."

I cautiously brought Princess round and walked her across the green to the gate by the stable, led her through to the paddock beyond and closed the gate. Now was the testing time. I turned the horse so that her head was over the gate, put my foot in the saddle and mounted. Princess stood as tame as anyone could wish.

From there on, the ride was a normal one for me of periodically going off track, managing to be caught by sleet squalls and arriving at fences with no gate to hand. I eventually reached KC with still half an hour's daylight left and was eminently satisfied.

Bill and Clara kindly provided lodging for the night. By morning, several inches of snow covered the ground and squalls were frequent. Princess, however, was quiet and started back to Douglas without trouble until we reached a hill and the gear slipped back. Princess got her head down and began bucking. She deposited me in one move but was not satisfied and kept bucking in circles until she got rid of the saddle. When she was calm, I tentatively approached her and took the rest of the gear off. Both her hind legs were cut. I left the gear scattered on the ground and led Princess back to Bill.

Bill inspected the cuts and found them to be no more than small nicks. He also looked at her feet and decided the hoofs should be tidied.

While Bill fetched hammer and knife and trimmed the horse's hoofs, Clara provided a restorative cup of coffee and suggested phoning Stanley radio from Douglas to have a 'safe return' message broadcast on the evening announcements. It was a sensible suggestion particularly as I had already caused trouble once that winter when high winds had prevented me recrossing the creek after a day visit from San Carlos. The resultant R/T calls between farm managers, interrupted during their Sunday break by employees enquiring after somebody with insufficient sense to watch the weather, had left me highly and rightly embarrassed. I promised to ensure a message was sent.

After the coffee, Bill accompanied me with Princess to the paddock where she had dumped me. He geared her and added a retaining girth to prevent the saddle slipping back again.

The gear kept position, Princess behaved herself and before long we were at the gate on top of Cerro Montevideo. I opened the gate, led the horse through, made sure the gate was fastened again and just stood there enjoying the view. There was an undisturbed snow carpet across the paddocks towards Douglas, and the mountains were shiny white right out to Mount Usborne on the horizon. The words of Good King Wenceslas described the scene exactly, 'deep and crisp and even' except it was morning squalls instead of bright moonlight. It was peaceful out there alone in the magical white of the fresh snow, an occasion to be savoured and remembered. It was exhilarating too but time was passing. I could not linger at the gate admiring the view.

I put my foot in the stirrup and lightly swung up. Princess shot away and I catapulted over her shoulder to thump down into the snow the other side.

Princess did not stop until she was a speck in the distance. The words that came to mind had nothing to do with marking footsteps well nor was the day exhilarating any more. Luckily Princess waited while I trudged after her and carefully remounted. I took great care after that. At each gate, I made sure the horse's head was across the fence before I remounted. Douglas was reached without further trouble and the 'safe return' message went out on the announcements.

The spell of weather was the coldest for nineteen years, dropping way below freezing point to a night minimum of minus seven degrees Celsius. The water-pipe to the settlement froze and water had to be carried from the well. The creek froze solid and people walked over to Teal Inlet Camp just for the novelty of it. Apart from that diversion the cold was nothing but a curse.

Winter work was seriously disrupted. It was the time when fencing was renewed, when miles of parallel wires had to be tensioned and fastened to heavy wooden posts. Navvy gangs should have been out in the farm caravans wherever fencing needed to be done. Fencing was gutty, muscle-building work; wielding pickaxe and shovel for holes, and sledge hammer to drive home the posts. It was piece-work. The more slog, the more pay. The more frost, the less chance to earn that pay.

The ice made the fencers' work impossible. They returned to flat rate wages at the cookhouse waiting for the weather to ease. The wait was longer than usual.

THE WIND-PUMP

When the weather eased at Port San Carlos, attention was turned to Cape Dolphin which was to be modernised with piped water. A shed stored the hardware; a Rayburn stove with back boiler, a bath, a W.C. pan, piping, crated parts for a wind-driven pump and a large cistern.

Rain water would still be collected off the roof but soon the ten-minute traipse to the spring in the valley for every bucket of drinking water would be over. No longer would there be the daily chore of emptying the loo bucket and renewing the chemicals. No longer would bath-night mean a tin tub in front of the range stoked to heat sufficient pans of water. All that would change and no one would regret it.

At modernisation time, Cape Dolphin was like a seaside guest-house in peak period although it was late winter and the guests were not on holiday. First Bill and Delhi arrived from the settlement. As shepherds they had nothing to do with the modernisation but were to assist the Cape shepherds in rounding up cattle along the coastal area. Then Stuart, a big, cheerful Scotsman, arrived with the crawler-tractor towing the farm sleigh with a cement mixer lashed to it. The sleigh was not an elegant structure but it could be taken safely across soft ground where a wheeled cart would become hopelessly bogged.

Stuart stayed the night and left for KC after breakfast. The sleigh and cement mixer graced the green awaiting the navvy gang.

Muzzie was not without visitors for long. By supper time, Tom, the handyman, had arrived with the big wheeled tractor and trailer bringing the three man navvy gang, Tom Dooley, Pat and Gyd ,another Scot, half the size of Stuart but just as cheerful.

Next morning, work began at six. First a tall, timber framework was built at the end of the house. The cistern was hoisted to the top and secured as a water-tower for the piped supply from the spring.

In the afternoon they began digging a large cess-pit. The tools for the job were the ever faithful pickaxe and shovel plus crowbar for obdurate patches. By the end of the day, the navvies were pretty well knee deep and quite satisfied with their progress.

After that, progress slowed. The men discovered that, lower down, the Cape Dolphin ground was well peppered with large rocks that required the crowbar and prolonged effort to shift. By the end of the morning session, knees were still at ground level and the only thing to have lowered noticeably was morale.

What was needed was a change of scene. This was providentially provided by the shepherds. Bill and Delhi had left earlier with a drove of cattle destined for the settlement. Rab and Keith were sorting out the Cape animals and selecting one for beef.

After dinner the groups went to their respective locations but neither had much luck. The rock was as resistant as ever and the big ox selected for beef had outmatched Keith's lasso for strength. Trailing yards of hide-rope, it sought refuge with the remainder of the cattle.

A hurried conference at the embryo cess-pit voted the provision of food as coming first in the natural order of things so they promptly downed tools and went to the aid of the shepherds. With such a number of helpers, it took twice as long to process the ox to beef and safely hang it at the palenque. Everybody agreed it was a job well done and deserving of an extended smoko. Late in the afternoon they returned to their crowbars.

That evening, Brook, the under-manager, phoned to say he would be riding out during the following day. Muzzie relayed the news to the navvies. The effect was electrifying.

Next morning, the rock's resistance crumbled almost to nothing. By the time Brook arrived, there was a cess-pit deep enough for any navvy gang's conscience.

Thursday, the excavation was completed and the cement mixer came into its own. Sand and shingle for it were supplied by the tractor and trailer. As the mixer chugged its way to the end of one load there was a break for a trip to the beaches for another. It all helped keep the work comfortably varied.

Finally, the navvies went down the valley to assemble the pump and wind vanes. A concrete and brick platform had to be built where the spring bubbled from the ground. Diverting the water presented a few headaches for the men but at last the platform was ready for the windmill.

Erecting the metal tower for the wind vanes that would provide power for the pump was like building with giant Meccano pieces but fitting the vanes at the top and connecting the long shaft accurately to the pumping mechanism at the spring took time and patience. There was no room for error and no ringing a firm for replacement pieces.

Eventually all was fitted and ready for testing. The brake was released. The wind vanes revolved, the shaft moved smoothly up and down and there was a steady gush of water. The pump was switched off while the final connection was made to the pipe taking the supply up the hill to the reservoir-tank. All was ready.

Tom took up position on the tower by the house. In the valley, Stan set his pump going. Soon there was a yell from Tom, "Water." Success!

22: The reservoir-tower beside the house. In the valley, the wind-vanes power the pump but Stan's wind charger stands idle, his R/T batteries are fully charged.

The gang left for the settlement and their place was taken by the plumber who would complete the inside work. He finished his considerable schedule and announced that the plumbing was ready for testing. Cold taps were turned and cold water ran. Hot taps too ran water equally cold and the toilet flushed. Time to stoke the Rayburn and see that all was well there. It was not long before the hot taps ran promisingly warm. In an hour the water was hot, no seams were bursting and Cape Dolphin was modernized.

Another leap forward was made during August. One of the evening radio announcements informed listeners that a supply of polio vaccine sufficient to inoculate 900 was in the islands. All those aged 20 or below would be treated. The first settlement to receive the vaccine would be Port San Carlos when the plane visited on the following Friday.

Friday proved a day of low cloud. No flying was possible.

Saturday was flying weather. The children and teenage employees collected at the cookhouse to await the arrival of the plane. Bonnie was there from Moss Side but nobody arrived from Cape Dolphin. The Cape horses had escaped from the paddock

The plane arrived with the doctor. The pilot waited while the doctor vaccinated the under-twenties and assured people that within a few months there would be enough for everyone. Vaccination completed, the doctor returned to the plane and continued to Fox Bay where more under-twenties were waiting.

At the end of the month the KC shepherds gathered the various flocks and drove them to the settlement for wigging, whereby any wool around the eyes was clipped clear to prevent wool blindness.

It was the swan song of the hand shears. Engineers from Stanley were busy installing machine shears at the wool-shed. Several snags were encountered but the installation was completed and all hands were mustered for the official opening. Mr Cameron thanked the engineers, made a joke about the old hand shears and switched on the engine. A new noise was added to the gamut of sounds associated with KC shearing. A demonstration was given to show the new techniques necessary. It was a valuable lesson for the shearers.

The following day wigging was completed with machine shears. In the summer shearing season, the men would be using them all day.

Swimming Horses

The next weekend I was due to be moved from KC to JB by Redwing because most of the horses were away on the tussac islands which lay just offshore along the creek between the settlement and Fanning Head. The tussac clumps provided both food and shelter being a mass of matted root growth up to two metres high crowned by drooping stems and leaves that remained green throughout the winter. The islands were an ideal winter stable complex because horses could be waded across at low tide and collected when needed.

Moving the teacher to JB by horse was burdensome at any time because it entailed the provision of a guide plus his horse. Both horses had to be swum across the creek before and after the move, a quarter mile swim each time across tidal water with a barrier of thick kelp fronds by the San Carlos shore. Mr Cameron preferred the winter moves to be by boat. He asked Fred and Pat to take Redwing round early Sunday when any who wished could have a day out.

Sunday brought filthy weather as snow squall chased snow squall along the valley and over the hills in a howling gale. Redwing remained at her moorings. It was decided that the move would have to be by horse after all as Fred and Pat could not be spared on Monday. Delhi would be guide while the other two continued with fencing repairs in the paddocks above the settlement.

Monday dawned clear but the wind was up with the sun. We needed to make a prompt start after breakfast and swim our horses across to the San Carlos side of the creek before the wind had a chance to strengthen much more.

The horses we needed were with the troop wintering on the tussac island. Delhi rode down there early while the tide was still low enough for wading. He was back with a group of horses driven into the corral by eight o'clock.

Delhi was going to use the pride of his troop, a large, lively horse in excellent condition. Strong willed and not easily caught, it gave a merry chase round and round the corral before Delhi managed to slip the bozal over its head and lead it out. I was allotted Fandango, a strong horse with a placid temperament.

Eileen, the governess, then approached and unforeseeable complications began. Eileen was booked for a flight to Goose Green to join Darwin on a trip to Punta Arenas in Chile for timber and horses. The morning R/T messages had included the familiar announcement that high winds were causing a revision of flight schedules. If the weather abated, the plane would call at KC during the afternoon but the Goose Green section was cancelled. Eileen's boat trip was in jeopardy. Her one chance would be to ride to Goose Green. Unfortunately, her horse was still on the island.

Eileen did not dally. Bill was crossing the green, heading home for breakfast.

She called across to him, "Bill, my flight's been cancelled. I'll have to ride to Goose Green or I'll miss the Darwin. Could you help me fetch Quickstep from the island? I'm sure the tide's low enough."

"Tide's really a bit high now, Eileen. You might be in luck. I'll ride down and see what I can do but it could take a couple of hours even if I find Quickstep."

"Thanks, Bill. I'm sure Delhi won't mind waiting for me."

Delhi had led his horse back to his house and secured it in the yard where it could not stray while he had breakfast.

Eileen met him at the gate, "Delhi, Bill's just riding down to fetch Quickstep for me. I shall miss the Darwin if I don't ride over and I don't know the track to JB. Can I ride with you and Ted, please?"

"If you don't know the track, I guess you'll have to, Eileen."

"Thanks, Delhi. Bill should be back soon after nine."

It was ten o'clock by the time Bill arrived back at the corral.

Eileen caught Quickstep, I collected Fandango from the green by Bill's house and we walked through the settlement to the creek. We were hardly there, when we had the surprise of seeing the Beaver come in low over the hills, bank round, trail spray as it touched down on the creek and taxi close to the shore.

23: The perils of boarding the plane; from rowing boat, to float, to rungs, to cabin.

Other people were obviously aware of the change because Fred had several passengers waiting in the boat ready to be rowed out. As the plane stopped, the boat set off and was soon alongside. There were the usual balancing acts as passengers transferred from the boat to the float of the plane and up the steep rungs into the cabin. The pilot took the outgoing mail, Fred pulled for the shore and the plane was ready for take off.

Although the inner part of the creek was fairly sheltered, there was enough wind for the plane to become airborne with a minimal take-off run. It rose low over the cookhouse and straight along the settlement, the noise reverberating around the valley. The sheep in the gorse squares took to their heels, rushing pell-mell into the corners where they stood perplexed, unable to move forward or to think of turning round. Within a minute the plane had gone and the settlement was quiet again.

Delhi had still not arrived. Fred suggested that we should begin swimming our two horses over. Quickstep was known to be of little trouble in the water. She could be taken without waiting for Delhi. I took the cabresto and sat in the stern of the boat while Fred pulled slowly away. Quickstep waded in. As the water reached her chest she hesitated a moment and then her feet were off the bottom and she was swimming steadily while Fred rowed carefully at her pace making for the small beach at the corner of the point where it was free of kelp. Fred reached the beach at last and Quickstep waded ashore.

By now Delhi was with Eileen on KC beach and the reason for his delay was clear, he had changed horses. His original one had certainly been lively when he caught it and would doubtless prove difficult in the water.

Fred rowed back for them. Steep, white-capped waves could be seen on the outer part of the creek running down to Hospital Point. The wind was blowing forcibly. It was small wonder that the plane had become airborne so quickly.

24: Persuading the horses to enter the water.

When Fred reached the other side, Delhi immediately stepped into the boat with both cabrestos in his hand; he was going to swim the two horses at once. Fandango tried to pull back but with Delhi's dogs barking and snapping at his heels he plunged into the water and both horses were soon off the bottom.

They proved strong swimmers and Fred was having trouble keeping the boat ahead of them.

25: The horses in mid channel between Port San Carlos and San Carlos shores.

Suddenly the reason was apparent. Seals. Seals certainly frequented the creek but it had been clear of them when Quickstep crossed. Yet here were several of them, their black heads raised as they quizzically surveyed the scene.

The horses were aware of the seals and were becoming increasingly agitated. Fred and Delhi were having difficulty maintaining a safe distance from the horses as seals surfaced first on one side then on the other. Suddenly one of the horses was right under the stern. The boat tipped, Delhi threw the cabrestos clear and Fred pulled like a man possessed.

The horses made a bee-line for land. Fred rowed hard for the shore and beached the boat. Delhi hurried to the place where they seemed likely to come ashore.

The two horses swam strongly but became entangled in the thick kelp. For a moment things seemed serious then they touched ground, struggled for a foothold among the rocks and crashed their way ashore. Delhi grabbed the cabrestos and led the horses off the beach to inspect them. Both had minor cuts but nothing more. Events could have taken a far more serious turn. Delhi, unusually quiet, seemed more upset than anybody.

Fred made yet another crossing for Eileen. By the time he returned, Delhi had declared the horses fit enough for riding. They went well and San Carlos was reached in time for dinner.

Not until later, when Delhi had returned to KC, did Eileen reveal the reason for his long delay. When the plane had taken off at KC and zoomed through the settlement valley scattering the sheep it had also panicked Delhi's horse. The frightened animal had leapt the garden gate and impaled its flank on a post the other side. Delhi had been obliged to destroy it. Small wonder he had been so quiet.

"PEWTURE MAN," HE MURMURED

Near gale-force squalls were scudding across San Carlos Bay and drumming against the window panes of Ray and Mary's sitting-room. Inside was snug and cosy but it was time to walk down to the dance-hall for the Saturday film. Mary put more peat on the fire and made sure the spark-guard was secure. Ray put the last of a pile of matches back into their box, his winnings from the afternoon's pontoon session. Patrick was revelling in the fact that he was being allowed to see the film instead of staying at home with a baby sitter. The film was to be *The Sea Shall Not Have Them* which seemed well worth the effort of leaving the warmth of the house. Everybody donned Wellingtons and waterproofs for the short walk down to the dance-hall and arrived there dripping puddles.

Wet outer coats were hung up, inner coats wrapped as warmly as possible and remarks exchanged about the hall heating system which was one black, upright paraffin lamp. As soon as the audience was complete, the projectionist began the first reel.

The drama of the film took the mind off the cold. People became engrossed in the intrigues of the agent carrying vital information back to England to help in the war against the Nazi powers.

The agent's progress inevitably suffered delay during each interval between reels while the new one was set on the projector and threaded through. The San Carlos delays were minimal, unlike Douglas Station where Vic showed the films. Vic's weekly bottle tended to cause difficulties over threading the film or directing the image towards the screen. Sometimes he had to accept defeat, "shuggest shomeone elsh showsit" and quietly retire to his room.

At San Carlos films, sobriety ruled. The second reel ran out as the hero, clutching his secret documents to his chest, huddled with his mates in their rubber dinghy on a restless North Sea. The audience waited quietly. The projectionist took the reel off, put it to one side and reached into the box for the next one. The box was empty. Despite all precautions, the San Carlos reel change had stalled.

Hall lights were switched on and people looked to see where the reel had been put. It had not been put anywhere. The third reel had never arrived and the show was over. Perhaps the sea was not to have them but as far as San Carlos could tell, the heroes were doomed to bob up and down on the North Sea for ever. People felt frustrated and suddenly very cold.

It was Jack who saved the evening by inviting everyone to his place for supper and a dance. Jack was the cook and 'his place' was the cookhouse. Jack was short and portly with a neat military moustache and a fringe of well-groomed hair about a spacious bald patch. He was a genial host and his occasional supper dances were quite a feature of winter life at San Carlos. They followed a set pattern of darts, skittles, supper and dance. Jack set-to in the galley to produce some food while the men cleared the tables from the living-room to make a dance floor.

That night, ladies teams played the men. When darts and skittles were over, the ladies retired to the galley and helped themselves to supper while the men had a quiet tot around the fire. When the ladies returned, the men had their supper.

Jack's suppers were always satisfying. On the table were a couple of loaves, baked by Jack the previous day, a dish containing pork which was a rarity in the cookhouse, a piece of salt beef, a pot of mustard and a tray of cakes. On the stove were two pots. One was of tea, stewing and neglected. The other was of coffee, percolating a strong, steadying black, guaranteed to keep a man on his feet.

After supper it was dance time. Music for the dance was provided by Jack's old wind-up gramophone. He quite rightly valued his gramophone and stack of 78's. After each record he rewound to an exact number of winds and religiously fitted a new needle. It was all done with great pomp and circumstance because it was Saturday evening, Jack's bottle was nowhere near as full as in the morning and Jack, woozy with whisky, was a paragon of attempted perfection.

As the record finished, the dancers waited patiently while Jack zealously counted the handle round and replaced his needle. That done, he set the turntable in motion and carefully lowered the needle onto the record. The band played its encore and the dance continued. Jack smiled happily; he was entertaining the settlement.

About one o'clock the ladies declared they had danced enough. The tables were put back into place, Jack was cordially thanked for his hospitality and everybody went home.

The squalls were still around in the morning. It was no day to go out unless obliged. Ray, being cowman, had to attend to the cows but after breakfast he settled to a morning's spinning. The wool was a dark brown from somebody's pet sheep. Ray had become a proficient spinner and Mary knitted the wool into socks, mittens or scarves. They were popular and she always had an order list. Mary had also bought a knitting machine and soon mastered it. She was able to reproduce intricate patterns in coloured wools for jerseys and other garments. Again she had a waiting list of customers.

In the afternoon Derek and his wife came over. They were next-door neighbours with a flat at the Big House where she was cook/ housekeeper. Later, we heard footsteps crunching unsteadily along the path. Jack arrived. He was in fine spirits but a little unsure of his feet. Ray and Mary invited him to stay for smoko and afterwards Jack issued a darts challenge, "Ted and I will challenge you two to 501 up. Best of three wins."

Ray had a dartboard on a large piece of boarding which could be hung in the kitchen. The challenge was accepted. The ladies were left to chat by the sitting-room fire and the men walked through to the kitchen.

Jack stumbled round the door and fell into the peat box.

"Pewture man!" he murmured. Jack's diction was always good but when he was slightly tipsy it was impeccable and his expressive "Pewture man" seemed charged with meaning.

"Pewture man," came again from the peat box.

The box was large and had been pretty well empty. Jack had finished right way up but sitting deep into it with his legs draped over the edge. All of his bulk was down among the peat sods and he could do no more than waggle his brown corduroyed legs and murmur

"Pewture man," until the laughter subsided and he was hauled out. He brushed himself down good naturedly and prepared to throw.

His dart for the bull ran out of momentum and flopped a metre short of the board. Jack retrieved the dart and declared the flight feathers were rather askew. He brushed his finger along them several times, announced himself satisfied and tried again.

Another of Jack's darts, aimed for double-top, skidded along the ceiling but others hit their target and the games kept surprisingly close.

For the fifteen minutes at the tag end of dusk when the manager had not yet switched on the generator for the lights and Ray's kitchen was virtually dark, the match became a game of chance for both sides and somehow Jack led his team to victory by two games to one.

Jack returned to his cookhouse after supper and the rest of the evening was passed playing Ludo in front of the sitting-room fire.

A Hundred Penguin Eggs

The days gradually lengthened into spring. The first of the lambs were born and riders were expected to be particularly quiet and careful when going through Camp that had ewes. The ewes were not folded for lambing and though the shepherd might be out from dawn to dusk he could not attend to all those that needed help. Dead lambs, even ewes were sometimes seen.

Where a lamb was orphaned the shepherd would attempt to put it to a ewe who had lost her lamb. If he succeeded, all was well and good. If not, the chances were he would place the lamb in front of him on the horse and return home with it as another pet for his wife or children to bottle feed.

Kelp gulls and turkey vultures helped keep the Camp clear of carcasses. As scavengers they were a boon. The down side was their propensity for taking the eyes and tongue of any sheep that was cast and too feeble to move in protest.

Spring did not bring a carpet of bright flowers. Colour was at a premium. There were flowers to be found, beautiful ones too, but, unless one knew where to search, most of them remained hidden in the white grass, the swamps or the stone-runs so the Camp kept its special low profile until the diddle-dee ripened.

Nor was the air full of the sound of birdsong. Yet territories were claimed and building went ahead. Most birds were left unmolested and only by chance were they disturbed. The exceptions were Upland geese and Gentoo penguins. Their eggs were a valued food resource preserved in water-glass for use through the year.

Upland geese began nest building about mid-September using grass or twigs lined with down. At weekends people went egging, spending the day searching for the tell-tale gander waiting off from the nest where the goose would be sitting almost hidden in diddle-dee or grass. The gander kept watch some distance from the nest. Sighting him did not lead immediately to the goose but it did provide a search area. The goose would sit tight especially if the eggs were near to hatching. Sometimes she could be practically trodden on before moving. 'Turned' eggs were left and the good ones carefully wrapped in grass for safe carrying. If enough eggs were collected, some would be pickled for winter use. Collecting the Uplands' eggs needed patience and a good eye.

The eggs of the Gentoo penguin were no trouble to collect but were heavy to transport in bulk. At KC, Delhi had a hundred penguin eggs for Ray at JB. One Sunday in late October Ray and I rode over to collect them. We hobbled the horses at the point and shouted for a boat. It was a calm day and voices carried well. Tom, the handyman, was on his way to the wool-shed and he signalled that he had heard. He brought the outboard motor dinghy over, its throaty engine announcing the arrival of visitors throughout the settlement.

The plan had been to pack the eggs and ride straight back but there was a bottle of whisky to be broached at the cookhouse. Somehow the hours slipped by until it was evening with the eggs still in the box at Delhi's.

The sun disappeared without setting and somebody noticed mist drifting in from the sound and already shrouding the Settlement Rocks. A start was made packing the eggs. By the time we finished it was nine o'clock and thoroughly dark.

Delhi's wife then provided a fried penguin egg supper for us which went down extremely well as we had missed dinner. As soon as supper was over, we made our way down through the settlement to the cookhouse. It was almost ten. Gyd kindly turned out and rowed us across the creek.

The horses were still there. We geared them carefully, making sure the eggs were securely loaded, and started up the first hill. It was a warm night and apart from the mist, which meant we could see little of the track, it was a pleasant ride. The horses were keen to get home and we were soon down in the central valley, through the streams and ascending the back of San Carlos hill.

There the climb was steeper and the horses slowed to a walk. We sat hunched in our maori coats half-asleep waiting for the rocks at the top so that we could get down the other side and be home. We did not even notice the summit but were happy enough to be descending. We stayed comfortably slouched while the horses picked their way down. They reached the bottom and began trotting again. It just remained to cross the peat banks to the gate behind Ray's house.

The horses trotted on but the gate did not materialize. After fifteen minutes trotting Ray reined in.

"You know, Ted, I don't think we've crossed the mountain."

"Oh?"

"We've been up and down again on the same side."

"Oh. Where are we?"

"We're around the Verde somewhere. We'll soon hit a fence and find out."

On we went and before long arrived at a fence. Ray reckoned we should turn right so we did and soon came to a gate. We passed through. The gate enabled us to get our bearings and having determined the direction of the settlement we set off at a fast trot. In ten minutes we were back at the gate.

"You know, Ted, we're lost."

"Yes."

"We'd better take it a bit slower."

We set off again at walking pace. Some half-an-hour later we reached a small pond. A sheep was on its back partially in the water. Ray dismounted to attend to it but it was an eyeless corpse. Ray rolled a cigarette instead. He took great pains to make it a good one since it was the last paper in his wallet and he would have to smoke it as long as possible. He lit it and off we went once more. The only thing visible was Ray's cigarette, a red glow-worm a little way ahead.

Before long we skirted another pond. That too had a dead sheep beside it. Then came a third pond with a third sheep. Ray stopped.

"I'm sure there's not a sheep at every pond, Ted. We might as well have a rest."

"Good."

We took the gear off, hobbled the horses and sat down. Ray was thirsty so broke one of the eggs and drank the white from it. He offered me one. I did not quite fancy it and preferred to lie back on my sheepskin cojinillo. It was warm there and a welcome change from sitting on a roundabout horse. I shut my eyes and relaxed. Penguin eggs and horses and eyeless sheep spun and ghosted round my head in a great woolly tiredness that floated off to a wonderful nothing.

"Shshsh! Wake up." Somebody had me by the shoulder, shaking me, "Careful Ted. Get up quietly."

I looked round, saw the reason and cautiously got to my feet. I had fallen asleep with the cabresto in my hand. Ray too had slept and had woken to see the horse's hind feet too close to my head for comfort.

It was turned four and we had become chilled while sleeping. We decided to move on. We alternated between riding and leading the horses but it made no difference, we could not shake off the pond with the wretched carcass until the mist was less dark and somewhere or other dawn was happening. We could see just a little further and the ground began to have shape and distance. We were able to move steadily forward instead of circling.

At last Ray announced that he knew where we were. He had felt pretty sure for some time but had thought it better not to say. It raised our spirits and we pushed the horses on a bit. We reached another fence and turned along it up the mountain. Soon the sun showed as a pale yellow disc above the mist. As we climbed higher the disc strengthened and in a few minutes we were riding in brilliant sunlight to the crest of the hill. Behind us our night valley was still swathed in mist. Below us lay San Carlos, glinting like a jewel with the sun reflecting off the white houses.

In another half-hour we were home drinking tea and trying lame excuses for losing our way. Ray had to rush off to the cows. It was six o'clock and he was normally well through milking by that time but for me it was still an early hour. I was able to unpack the eggs at leisure before going off to light the school room fire.

Trackside Rendezvous

When I went out to Sussex the next Saturday, the story of the egg-collecting ride was already there. The boys reckoned that if I could not find something as big as San Carlos I would certainly never find anything as small as a nest. Consequently, they organised a fortnight of nesting expeditions for me.

The boys were sharp-eyed and if a nest was there, they found it. At Hell's Kitchen, a steep-sided gully where one of the streams entered the creek, they found a robin's nest with a full clutch of four blue-white eggs. Strictly speaking, the robin was a long-tailed meadowlark with the bearing of a starling but it had such a stunningly red breast it was a robin to everyone. Thrush, skylark, dotterel, finch; somehow the nests were discovered. Yet at no time did the boys attempt to collect the eggs. The sport was in being sharp-eyed and alert enough to find the nest.

One morning their alertness was more than usually useful. People had roused early. Frank was busy at the peat banks cutting his quota of fuel, the boys were outside making the most of their free time before school and the remainder of the adults were in the kitchen enjoying an early morning cup of tea.

Suddenly Sydney burst straight into the room fully booted, an absolute taboo. Something had to be wrong.

"Mum, there's an awful lot of smoke coming from the sitting-room chimney."

Not even Sydney could joke like that. A rush was made for the sitting-room.

"Sand, Ellen. Fetch the sand!" screamed Jean, and Ellen fled down the passage.

When the door was opened the smell of soot filled the air. There was no billowing smoke or threatening flame from the fireplace but the room was exceptionally hot. The chimney was afire, about that there could be no doubt, and it must have been alight some time. Without more ado we removed the burning sods from the grate, made a deal of smoky, acrid fumes and took the whole lot outside in the ash-pan.

Thick black smoke was issuing from the chimney and pluming into the sky. Ellen had the sand. Tubby obtained the ladder stored underneath the brick piers supporting the house. He placed it against the guttering. I climbed the ladder, took two quick paces and a lunge to grab hold of the roof ridge and sat astride it. Tubby followed up the ladder and passed me a pan of sand. I shot it down the chimney. The plume of smoke faltered and thinned. Another pan of sand and the smoke ceased altogether. There were concerted sighs of relief.

At that point Frank rode round the hill smiling and outwardly calm, "I saw the smoke from the peat bank and wondered what was wrong."

"Just the chimney caught fire," answered Sydney. As far as he was concerned it was just that. What might have happened did not enter his mind.

We went back inside to check the sitting-room. The pans of sand, whether or not they had been responsible for putting out the fire, had certainly brought the soot down. The room had soft black snowflakes still eddying and settling on the chairs, the table, the carpet, everywhere. In the grate lay a mound of soot with trickles still descending from the chimney.

Clearing up continued well into the second day. When the sitting-room was in use again, people felt an overpowering urge to pop in and check the fire once more, just in case.

Tubby was the next to give Jean palpitations. He had a bike, old and battered with neither tyres nor brakes. There was a tempting slope on the hill above the house which gave him the chance to delight in speeds otherwise unobtainable by his machine. He would swoop down the hill, across the house paddock to the back door and slide to a halt with the help of his own ingenious braking system.

Perhaps it was spring madness that led Tubby to career down more crazily than usual. Perhaps it was the joy of having his two older brothers, David and Lars, out on holiday with him. Whatever the cause, he climaxed his evening's exploits with a wilder than ever descent, finishing with a broadside that saw the front wheel buckled beyond redemption and Tubby in a painful heap by the back door.

Tubby was not talkative at the best of times. Now he was silent and white. His mother took him indoors. His forearm was badly swollen and tender. Jean put the arm in a sling and made him as comfortable as possible. Medical attention was imperative.

Ellen phoned the settlement and the settlement phoned the doctor at Darwin. An appointment was made for the following day. The doctor was due at San Carlos settlement to administer polio inoculations to adults. He would give the Sussex household theirs and examine Tubby's arm at the iron gate where the Darwin/San Carlos track crossed Sussex Mountain.

Tubby stoically maintained the arm was not too bad but the sooner he saw the doctor the happier everyone would be. It was a long night for both Tubby and his mother.

In the morning people were up early, washed and breakfasted, anxious not to be late. By 9.30 they were ready at the gate. The doctor was expected in his Land Rover about ten o'clock.

It was the first of November, All Saints Day, and the glorious weather must have been provided by one of them. The gate was the regular place to re-gear horses before descending the mountain and was a popular 'totting' stop for the riders as half-a-dozen whisky and gin bottles stuck neck-down by some ferns bore witness.

The ferns formed comfortable couches and became the doctor's waiting room. The morning was warm, the view peaceful. Watch was kept for the Rover but nothing disturbed the quiet. The curve of the hill hid the nearer part of the track. Lower down, the brown line wound through gullies to the creek and beyond the horizon to Darwin and Goose Green.

The headwaters of the creek shimmered along the dark shore-line. Time idled by. The ferns no longer seemed so comfortable and shade became more attractive than sun. Still there was no sign of movement along the track, the white sheep-dots grazed undisturbed. Only at the creek was there any change where the dark margin of wet rock imperceptibly lowered with the falling tide.

Sydney had boasted that he was the sharpest-eyed and would spot the Rover first. By noon his enthusiasm had waned and he changed his challenge to being the best eye in throwing. Frank and Tubby remained quietly in the shade while the others built a small pyramid of stones on the gate-post and shied missiles at it. Sydney proved unassailable, but he missed seeing the Rover. Frank, patiently waiting, caught sight of something on the far side of the creek, a small puff-ball of dust. Everyone jerked to life. The doctor was on his way.

The puff-ball drew to the edge of the creek and became a silver cascade crossing the shallow water. For a while it was hidden in a valley, then a dust cloud arose on a ridge. A smudge in the dust became the Rover, gradually progressing through a succession of humps and valleys until at last it reached Sussex Mountain and began the zigzag climb.

Tubby gave a sigh of relief, Sydney opened the gate wide. The Rover was lost to view again in dead-ground but the noise of the engine became louder and nearer until the vehicle finally rounded the hill, passed through the open gate and stopped. The doctor had arrived.

Wasting no time, he produced a flask containing the vaccine.

"Right, everyone. I need to be quick in administering the polio vaccine. Adults form a line, please. Left sleeve well up."

The doctor began his injections, his companion filmed proceedings and David fainted. He soon revived and was placed by the rocks while the casualties were seen.

First was Tubby with his swollen arm. A thorough examination showed it to be a fracture but nothing out of position. The arm needed the support of a plaster. From the back of the Rover the doctor produced a few rolls of plaster of Paris which simply had to be soaked in cold water and bound on the arm. There was one snag; no water. The problem was not insurmountable. A couple of whisky bottles from the ferns were re-cycled and Sydney set off down the hill to find a stream.

Meanwhile, the doctor turned his attention to Frank who had a painful thigh. His horse had fallen with him while wading through the stream at Hell's Kitchen. Having deposited Frank in the water, the horse had trodden on his leg. The doctor assured him he had nothing worse than a badly bruised muscle which would soon become easier.

When Sydney returned, somewhat out of breath, with his whisky bottles filled with brown peat-stained water, the doctor was able to deal with Tubby's arm. The water was emptied into a tin, the bandages were soaked and the broken arm was securely bound. As soon as the bandages dried, Tubby would have a firm plaster.

The doctor closed his bag, the photographer put his camera away and surgery was over for the day. The Rover departed for San Carlos.

Frank shut the gate, stuck the bottles back beside the ferns and led the way home.

SMELLY, GREASY SHEEP

Towards the end of November when the lambs were strong and well-established, lamb-marking took place. The lambs were ear marked, their tails docked and their suitability as potential breeding rams decided. It was work essentially done early in the day and the men had to start at dawn. It involved the shepherds, the under-manager and the manager himself.

By four o'clock they were up and gearing the horses. Two 15-year-olds in their first year of shepherding were net-boys in charge of the two long 'trapping nets', the breakfast rations and the large, black iron kettle, all of which were loaded on an extra horse.

The shepherds mounted, called their dogs to heel and without more ado were away to Race Point Paddock.

At three places around Race Point there were rectangular 'marking pens' fenced on three sides only. The shepherds began driving the ewes and lambs towards the first of these while the two net-boys rode straight to it and prepared their nets.

A net was tied to each side of the open end of the pen and extended at an angle away from it to form a funnel. The boys laid the nets in the grass so that they were completely hidden. When the sounds of the drive drew near, the boys lay flat.

The flock was slowly driven between them. If a sheep seemed about to wander, the net was shaken to deter it. Once the flock was past, the boys rose to their feet and brought the nets round to complete the pen. The shepherds then secured a section of the sheep in a smaller enclosure and marking could begin.

Each lamb was caught and seated on a bar along one side of the enclosure. Mr Cameron selected the best of the males to be left as future breeding rams and the others were rubber ringed to effect castration. Bill, as head shepherd, cut the station and age marks in

17: Tony, Muzzie, Stan and Jenny leave Port San Carlos and head home to Cape Dolphin, a ride of about 2½ hours. The gorse is coming into bloom. On the right is the Big House.

18: Looking back from Cape Dolphin across the sand bay and Smylies Village towards Port San Carlos. Upland geese are grazing on the green.

19: Port San Carlos. The children's Christmas party in the Big House. Jellies, crackers, Christmas cake and more, plus Father Christmas waiting in the wings.

20: Jenny and Tony with a welcome addition of goslings for the larder. Jenny is carrying bolas around her neck. Tony has his faithful lasso.

21: Tom Dooley steer riding at San Carlos Centenary Sports. In the background are the judges and the mounted assistants ready to help riders if necessary.

22: The gate opened and out rode Oscar, his hat poised obligingly for the camera. By the creek is Big John's jeep that bogged so often on the trip from Stanley.

23: Brook piloting Redwing up the creek for a fishing afternoon. He was rewarded with the biggest catch of the afternoon.

24: Gavin displays his dad's super fish, 5½ pounds of tasty trout duped by Brook's spinning minnow.

the lamb's ear and Brook, as under-manager, docked its tail. It was messy, smelly and very necessary work for which cool weather was appreciated.

When no more lambs were left in the small enclosure the ewes were released one by one so that an accurate count could be made. Choral chaos ensued as bleating ewes located their bleating off-spring amidst protests voiced by the next group entering the enclosure.

Once the last of the sheep were in, some of the shepherds commenced gathering again while the boys coiled their nets and moved on to the next pen. There they set the nets and then made a diddle-dee fire, filled the kettle from a spring and set it on the fire to boil. They returned to their nets and when the sheep were safely penned everyone stopped for food. Cold roast-mutton ribs and hunks of bread washed down with mugs of hot, kettle-brewed coffee made a welcome breakfast. It was half-past seven and the sun's strengthening warmth was beginning to accentuate the odour of sheep and blood.

By the time the third and final pen was reached the sun was high in the sky and the smells were a stench. With great relief the last ewe was released, the nets were coiled and the homeward ride began.

26: Lamb marking breakfast by the diddle-dee fire. Rab, Bill, Keith and Pat.

When Mr Cameron reached the settlement he could compare the tally of ewes and lambs' tails to work out a lambing percentage. If 70 per cent of the ewes had lambed successfully he would be pleased.

The end of November also saw the beginning of shearing which would last until February, by which time the men of KC would have shorn their way through 27,000 sheep

First, a flock had to be gathered and drafted. Gathering too was begun early in the morning, the shepherds setting off together, each with his several dogs, then fanning out to comb a particular section of Camp. Once at the far end of his area, the shepherd worked back steadily collecting sheep from the favoured feeding spots.

From all around were whistles and calls of shepherds instructing their dogs, some sent to winkle out more sheep, others to keep the group moving in the right direction. Through the day, small flocks gradually enlarged. The whistles, shouts, barking and bleating became noisier as shepherd met with shepherd. When the last groups merged, the completed flock was ready for the drive back to the settlement.

Once the sheep reached the settlement they had to be drafted into specific groups. Drafting was done at a 'race', a narrow corridor

27: The gathered flock being drafted at San Carlos wool shed.

along which the sheep were moved in single file to swing gates leading to various pens. The shepherd had to note the cuts in the sheep's ears and set the gates to make sure that each sheep finished in the correct pen. It was a job for an experienced man.

Each evening the shearing shed pens were filled ready for the morning to ensure dry, greasy sheep for better shearing.

28: Delhi and Pat filling the KC sheep pens.

Inside the shed there were smaller pens beside the shearing floor. On the other side of the floor, sack-covered openings gave entrance to the pens for shorn sheep. Each man had his own pen because his pay depended on the number of sheep he sheared. At the end of the floor were slatted tables where the fleeces would be graded and stored in bins until they were baled at the hydraulic press ready for shipment to the U.K.

At six o'clock the engine was started and put in gear. The long axle above the shearers began revolving and work commenced. The shearer pushed through the door of the crowded pen, seized a sheep behind the forelegs, tipped it onto its hind legs and backed out onto the floor, the door banging shut again. He positioned the sheep between his knees, pulled apart the wool on its belly, tugged at the rope switch to start the shears, grabbed them and began shearing so that the fleece fell away in one unbroken blanket.

The shorn sheep was pushed through the sack-covered opening and the shearer turned to collect another. Into the pen, seize a sheep, back it out, part the wool, tug and grab the shears and carry on shearing, "Keep still, you woolly legged ———," while sweat poured, the fleece fell away and the shorn sheep disappeared through the sacking. And then back for another; sheep after sheep after smelly, greasy sheep.

29: The KC shearing gang at work; Tom Dooley, Keith, Pat and Bill.

The wool boy collected each fleece, layered it carefully and threw it on the slatted table so that it spread out fully, dirty side up for the inspection of the grader. The grader picked off the dirty edges, checked the fibre for quality, twisted some into a rope, folded the fleece in, tied it with the rope and threw it in the appropriate storage bin.

There was no five minutes off, no stopping for a quick breather or chat. As soon as one sheep was shorn, the shearer took another; as soon as one fleece had been bundled, another was on the table. The wool-boy hurried from shearer to shearer collecting each fleece as it left the sheep and keeping the floor swept clean. If a sheep was accidentally cut, the woolboy had to stop whatever he was doing and take the tar pot for the shearer to treat the wound.

The day lasted twelve long, hot hours in five sessions of sweat in the noise and smell of oily machines and sheep. When the engine finally stopped, the frenzy calmed and a wonderful peace settled on the shed. The only sounds were the occasional bleating of sheep in the pens and the shuffling of their feet on the hollow wooden floor.

The working day was over and men made for baths, supper, long drinks of tea, a short relaxation and early bed ready for the next six o'clock engine.

30: Night shift. KC wool; shorn, graded, baled and loaded for the U.K.

Santa by Daylight

In the midst of the hectic days of the shearing season there was always the welcome break of Christmas. Many people liked to go to Stanley for the festivities which included the annual race meeting and sports. Others preferred to stay at home. Stan and Muzzie kindly invited me to spend Christmas with them at Cape Dolphin.

Christmas is Christmas whether it is mid-winter or high summer. For the housewife it is the same seasonal baking, the pudding, cakes and mince-pies. For the children there are the same long days of waiting.

For Tony and Jenny at the Cape, they were outside days spent carting peat home, riding, helping with the animals or just playing in the sands and chasing Upland geese 'shedders'. Shedders had moulted their flight feathers and were temporarily unable to fly. During December vast numbers grazed on the greens behind the Cape sands as if fattening themselves as a Christmas offering.

The geese were certainly vulnerable at that time but they showed a surprising turn of speed if they were obliged to run. They seemed able to find just enough acceleration to leave a chasing child clutching air or belly flopping in their wake. The birds would scuttle off the greens, across the sands and into the waves in a flurry of legs and wings. Once seaborne they sat back to bob and paddle nonchalantly until the children became tired of getting cold legs in the surf and left them alone.

As Christmas Day drew near, there were presents to wrap, cards to write and decorations to be festooned throughout the house. Finally came the expedition for a bunch of fragrant vanilla daisies to be set in a vase on the sitting-room table.

Christmas Eve was still in twilight at ten o'clock by which time the children had long been in bed. Carols had been listened to on the radio and empty pillow cases taken upstairs. The penultimate window on the Advent Calendar was open wide. All was set for the wonder and thrill of Christmas Day.

In the kitchen, Santa finished a few household chores and then, when things seemed quiet overhead, two bundles of packages were produced and slipped as silently as parcels will allow into two more pillow cases. They were placed under the table, the night drink cups were washed and the fire safely banked. Time for bed. The kitchen clock ticked and the 'cuckoo' called the quarters to a sleeping house.

As the first suggestions of dawn paled the rooms, a few quiet, furtive scuffles happened. Children were on the move. Tiptoes descended the stairs, pitter-pattered along the passage and paused. The handle of the kitchen door fidgeted a little and an enthralled sigh escaped. Something rustled across the floor, bumped softly up the stairs and slid along the landing. Wrapping-paper crackled. A few notes came from a mouth-organ. A second joined in with more gusto and brought a commanding thump against the wall. The music stopped and the house settled back to sleep.

It was grey cloud and eight o'clock before anyone stirred again. Santa got up, raked the fire and put the kettle on for tea. Others trooped in and Merry Christmas was wished all round. Adult presents were exchanged and the children's gifts inspected in detail.

The calves had their own gift with all 17 of them put to the cows to take as much milk as they wanted. Muzzie was not spending Christmas Day milking cows. The children on the other hand did have one chore as they both had pet lambs and pet lambs could not be ignored.

After breakfast the adults listened to the service from Stanley Cathedral and afterwards the children were called from their presents and everyone listened to the Queen's speech.

In KC settlement, people followed up the Queen's speech by gathering at the Big House for a short carol service. From there the cookhouse men visited each house in turn and joined the family for a Christmas toast. Each house invited one of the men to eat with them and gave him as tasty a meal as he could wish.

At Cape Dolphin the Christmas meat was a young lamb; sweet,

31: The Cape Dolphin pet lambs have their Christmas milk.

succulent and greed-inducing. The vegetables were straight from Stan's garden and the Christmas pudding was coated with thick cream from the Cape cows.

The adults voted for a lazy afternoon. The children took themselves off for more energetic pursuits.

Lazy afternoon was followed by Christmas tea and crackers. Everybody crossed hands to pull the crackers as one. Crackers crackled and wrappings burst. People perched paper hats on their head, read out the ridiculous jokes and searched for gifts lost in the gaudy litter among the plates. Christmas tea with the sun still high in the sky and the little crib in the Advent calendar announcing, "Christmas is Christmas wherever you are".

When the dishes were cleared away and the calves penned for the night, people sat around the fire and chatted of other Christmases and yawned and stretched back comfortably to gaze into memories dancing in the peat flames. Conversation ceased. It had been a long and happy day but now bed was calling. By the time darkness settled, the clock was again ticking to a sleeping house.

Boxing Day dawned bright and sunny. Morning was given over to milking and household chores but an afternoon ride was planned.

While Muzzie prepared an early dinner the children stabled the horses; Fanny, O'Neil, Tangle, Tom and Topsy, a little Shetland. The ride would be a circular one visiting the haunts of seals on the west of the peninsula and crossing to the east for penguin rookeries.

It was an easy-going afternoon, jogging along leisurely with no grumbling rumble of summer traffic or hurly-burly of holiday crowds. Only the sheep shared the countryside and they blended almost unnoticed with the white grass.

The seals were at the expected beach doing the expected thing of lazing on the rocks. There were small cliffs and a valley running down to the beach. The horses sensed the presence of the seals and became restless, their nostrils quivering and eyes showing white. Stan and Muzzie stayed with them and moved to the next valley while the children took me to inspect the seals.

Stan's dogs found something in the second valley too. They were barking vociferously and he was having to call them off. We left the seals and walked back to find out what the fuss was about.

Muzzie's voice rang out, "Whoa there, Tangle. Whoa, stop. Stop you silly thing. Come back. Stan, they're away."

We were in time to see Tangle and O'Neil go over the hill at a canter. Stan and Muzzie too were watching them and it had nearly been a case of watching four go. When Stan had gone to call off his dogs, Muzzie had been tightening the gear on Fanny and holding the cabrestos of the other four. She accidentally let them fall and that had been enough for Tangle and O'Neil; off they went. Tom and Topsy the Shetland had been slower in the uptake and Muzzie had managed to grab their cabrestos as they moved away.

"I'll get them," said Tony. He mounted Tom and went off in hot pursuit followed by Jenny on Topsy. When Muzzie finished gearing Fanny, she too went. Stan and I sat on the cliffs and watched the seals lazing on the beach.

In half an hour the others returned. Tony, true to his word, had stopped the horses by heading them off until Muzzie arrived to help lead them back. Gear was reorganised and the outing continued to the other side of the promontory where there was a Gentoo penguin rookery on top of the cliffs.

32: The Gentoo Penguin Rookery at Cape Dolphin. Overhead, a skua waits to rob.

The Gentoos gazed and quarrelled, poked at their neighbours and made sudden beaky lunges to snatch material from a next-door nest to add to their own which was being similarly depleted from the other side. There were all stages of development from eggs, through small, newly hatched chicks, to ragged adolescent birds trying to nestle into their parent's feathers.

Gliding above the rookery, on broad spread wings, were brown skuas ever watchful for the opportunity to rob an unguarded nest of its egg or nestling. One egg was so large it had to be a double-yolk so we became robbers ourselves and took the egg as a curiosity. It would never have become penguin.

We left the Gentoos to their squabbles and carried on to the Jackass nesting site. We could hear the braying of the birds well before we reached the place. The horses became so uneasy that we left them tethered to a gate while we completed the journey on foot. The ground was riddled with the burrows of nesting penguins. Some of the holes were long, while in some the bird was visible peering forward from its nest, neck extended, ready to peck viciously at anything approaching too near.

The Jackasses had drainage problems, the smell was abominable.

33: Jackass penguins on Cape Sands free from drainage problems of the nest.

Since nobody expressed a wish to linger, we left them braying to each other, or to us, whichever it was, and went back to the horses.

During the day the dogs had gone to one or two cast sheep. Stan had set them on their feet again. Near the rookery was a dead one. Stan stopped to skin it. Tony stayed to help. The rest of us continued.

Over by a hill a lone cow stood watching our progress. Muzzie reined in.

"That's Peggy!" she declared, "She must have a calf stowed away somewhere."

We went to investigate. Sure enough, the calf was curled among some diddle-dee well hidden from view. It could not have been more than a day or two old and Muzzie decided it was too young to be moved so cow and calf were left in peace.

In the next valley was another cow, Eve, with a calf about a week old, a bull calf promptly named Adam. Adam was a strong calf. He and his mother were slowly driven towards home.

On the way, a large cut of cattle with calves among them was seen and Muzzie decided the whole group should be brought along. The cows refused to move and Eve strongly objected to joining them. As cowhands we were not doing too well. Luckily Stan and Tony reappeared and the picture quickly changed.

Stan sent the dogs to move Eve and progress began. Cattle bellowed, dogs barked, people shouted and the quiet day was gone. A cow broke away and half a dozen dogs were on to it, snapping about its heels until it cavorted its way back into the herd.

The activity was great but the pace was slow to allow for the young calves. Once the first flurries of noise abated, the cattle resigned themselves to movement and the dogs were content to let them amble. Then the children produced their Christmas harmonicas and began a puff-blow polka to cheer the party on its way.

Eventually the house was reached and the cattle penned at the corral. There, Muzzie separated the cows with calves, including Brown who was obviously soon to calve, and put them in a small paddock. The remainder were turned loose again to make their way at considerable speed back to their grazing ground.

For the adults, the Christmas festivities were over. The children had one more treat in store, the KC Christmas party.

34: Chocolate éclairs and meringues oozing cream.

When the day came, mothers and children made their way through the settlement to the Big House. It was a wonderful occasion of best clothes and, if parents were to be obeyed, a mantle of decorum.

At the Big House, Mr and Mrs Cameron welcomed their guests.

Safely inside, everyone could relax. Mothers sat and indulged in a chat and a joke, keeping a wary eye on their offspring. The children were children together, manager's and farm worker's, enjoying the occasion and eyeing the feast.

The long dining table was laden with jellies, pastries, sandwiches and cakes. Fruit tarts, gingerbread, iced chocolate cakes, fairy cakes, éclairs and meringues oozing cream lay in mouth-watering array. In the centre stood the candled Christmas cake and by every plate was a cracker.

At one end of the room was the Christmas tree. Above the fireplace at the other end, a portrait of great-grandfather Cameron, founder of the farm, looked down with Victorian approval.

The children ate their fill, mothers sipped tea and looked on contentedly; no child was allowing excitement to spoil the day.

With the food gone, Father Christmas played his part, a gift for each child from the grotto of Mr and Mrs Cameron. The party was over; a happy day for everyone.

CENTENARY CELEBRATIONS

In the new year, San Carlos had another celebration, the farm centenary. Three days of events had been planned to coincide with the end of the shearing season so that as many people as possible could participate. Most North Camp farms were having a full week's holiday to enable visitors to travel at leisure and enjoy the celebrations to the full.

When the time came, nearly everyone from KC went, leaving only Bill's and Tom's families there along with Murdo and his wife, Elizabeth. Fred took some round on Redwing while Tom ferried the rest across the creek for the walk over the mountains. Douglas Station shepherds acted as guides for riders from Stanley. A few of the Douglas men made the long sea trip round Cape Dolphin Promontory in their farm boat Seagull. From the south, groups of Darwin and Goose Green riders arrived throughout the afternoon. Last of all, a small convoy of Land Rovers drove in, having had a chequered journey from Stanley and Fitzroy.

By the Monday evening, San Carlos was overflowing with visitors and at bedtime every room, except the bathrooms, became a dormitory so that somehow or other a sleeping place was found for every guest.

Tuesday was horse-racing day. Because the paddocks in the immediate vicinity of the settlement were too hilly for racing, a course had been marked off along Burnt Camp between the mountain and the creek.

A tractor and trailer provided a bus service for the spectators. If it was not quite Epsom Downs on Derby Day, it was still a festive occasion. Instead of a stand beside the finishing post, there was wire fencing to keep people off the final 300 metres. The first part of the course was marked by wooden posts. There were no tic-tac men or bookies shouting the odds but you could have a flutter on the tote and a tot at the bar when your throat felt dry.

The races provided plenty of competition, some exciting finishes and acute embarrassment for the jockey whose mount started so quickly he found himself out of his saddle and astride the horse's rump where he was still located as the horse passed the post, comfortably last but cheered loudly by the laughing spectators. He gained as much applause as the winner.

It was late afternoon by the time the final race was decided. The tractor bus then took back anybody who had not decided that walking was far preferable to being jolted to pieces across San Carlos paddocks.

After supper, people spruced up for the first of the dances. Because the dance hall was far too small for such a gathering, one end of the wool-shed had been converted by dismantling the wool bins and erecting canvas screening to separate the ball room from the shearing floor. The surface was very respectable and the draught under the screening encouraged people to dance rather than sit chatting on the benches round the edges. At refreshment time there was an invigorating walk to the cookhouse after which it was back to the music until four o'clock, then home for a few hours' sleep to recharge for the gymkhana events.

The gymkhana took place in one of the narrow settlement paddocks sloping up to the hills. The weather was glorious, a day of clear blue skies without the slightest breath of wind. Everybody determined to make the most of it. There was a mixture of foot and riding events set under way with spar-boxing where opponents sat astride a pole and whacked at each other with stuffed bagging 'battle-axes' until one contestant suddenly inverted like a sloth when a final whack on the hands normally dispatched him to the ground.

The tug-of-war matched North of Mount Usborne against the South in best of three pulls competitions. The South men won by two pulls to one. It was up to the North ladies to square the match. At one pull each, it reached a nail biting climax. In the final pull, the North ladies dug their heels deep, found a new source of strength, hauled the opposition over the line and collapsed in a triumphant heap. Only the anchor lady at the back of the team could account for their power; Stan, the perfect gentleman, had lent the ladies a hand in their time of need.

Next were mile and half-mile races up and down the hillside to give wind the edge over muscle. Plenty of competitors set out but the upward slope became steep and the downward one played havoc with tired feet to sift the reveller from the youthful fit. In an unexpectedly close finish, the glory of the mountain mile victory went to Patrick, an up and coming announcer from Stanley Radio Station.

Most hotly contested of the foot events was 'Stepping the Hundred Yards' where men had to pace out the correct distance. 100 yards was the standard length of a peat bank. A tape was the most accurate way of measuring it but years of experience taught a peat-cutter to estimate his bank's length. This event would sort the men from the boys.

Each contestant took a peg, paced his hundred yards, pushed his marker into the ground at the exact spot and considered the errors of his competitors. When the final peg was in place, the judges took their tape and measured the official 100 yards. Woe it was. A tape too short for some, too long for others, with the judges in error either way. Faces expressed disbelief. Just one man stood with a smile of triumph. He had got it right; almost.

Such was the esteem of the 100 Yards that several erroneous pacers felt their noses a little off centre. The rules for the wheelbarrow race made that the order of the day and stipulated men's noses to the ground and women in the driving seat. Nobody could take that too seriously and soon the pairs were drawn up and ready at the line. The starter's flag fell and the race was under way. It saw hard driving, some total write-offs and general good humour for all of the participants. Those who had not collapsed during the race did so as they finished, which was the signal for refreshments all round in readiness for the final foot event of the day.

This event was strictly ladies only. No man was allowed to enter, no man dared interfere. It was 'Chase the Rooster'. A dozen ladies were game enough. Off went the rooster and off went the chasers in pursuit to the cheers and laughter of the men as first one contestant and then another, in unladylike poise, just failed to grab the fleeing bird. At last a lunging figure held fast to its leg and there, prostrate on the ground, was the winner, Marj from Douglas Station, lying exhausted but triumphant with the rooster safely in her hands. Marj rose to her feet, the rooster was returned to seek solace amongst its hens and people turned to the next horse event.

The riding provided plenty of entertainment and a few worrying moments. In the 'Dummy Race' the horse had to contend with a huge dummy in front of the rider and the noise of exploding firecrackers and empty oil drum 'canon'. The race climaxed to a short-head victory for a visitor from Goose Green but Big John received a nasty kick above the knee.

The 'Gear Race' left several riders injured. Jockeys had to ride bareback along the course, sort out their gear from a central jumble, gear their horse and race back to the finish. Competition was so intense that several jockeys threw caution to the wind, grabbed their gear, put it across the horse and leapt aboard without tightening the cincha in their quest to be first past the post. Two of them paid with heavy falls and became limping spectators for the rest of the day.

That evening, the wool-shed was so cold for the dance that its progress depended on the determination of the dancers. They managed into the small hours when the M.C. decided that bed was best.

35: San Carlos cattle corralled before the steer riding.

Another clear dawn heralded the final day of celebrations, steer riding day. The animals had been brought down from the hills several days previously. Now they were in the corral on the small headland between the Big House and the creek.

A bullock was lassoed and driven into the narrow race at the corner of the corral. Men banded it with strips of hide, one round the shoulders and under the belly and one back under the tail.

A rider lowered himself onto the bullock, took tight hold of the band around its shoulders and sang out that he was ready. The gate was opened and out went the bullock, bucking for all it was worth, determined to dump whatever was on its back. For the rider, it was three bucks, mid-air and the hard ground.

I had the doubtful honour of being dumped the quickest, two paces beyond the gate, in marked contrast to Tom Dooley who had two rides and stayed aboard for both. Steer riding brought the celebrations to a close.

The following day the weather broke, the rain was torrential and people returning home were soaked before they were clear of the settlement. Some preferred to hang on another day so a final dance was held; this time in the dance hall. It proved the best dance of the lot. The hall was warm, Mr Bonner made a magnificent entry blazing away on a bugle, two of his guests were in ridiculous fancy dress and dancers took their cue to make it an evening to remember.

The next morning brought everyone down to earth with a bump. John from Wreck Point had an urgent message to go to KC. His father, Murdo, was seriously ill. The next day Murdo died.

On the Monday, people assembled at KC for the funeral. At a quiet service in the small cemetery on the hill beside the creek, they laid Murdo to rest. Wreaths of Falkland flowers marked the passing of a respected islander.

FISHERMAN'S DELIGHT

Sydney introduced me to fishing out at one of the Sussex streams. His tackle was a meat-baited hook on a short length of string. He dangled it in the water and moments later pulled it up with a minnow sucking hard at the meat. When he tired of catching minnows and returning them to the stream, he took me on a wild strawberry hunt. It was equally productive and provided a tasty smoko on a Sussex hillside.

For serious coarse fishing, a hand-line and hook was the most economical system. Equipment was minimal and returns could be great. The main quarry were mullet coming in on the rising tide where streams entered the sea. Head of the Bay was a favourite spot and, on a good day, mutton bait would bring in fish after fish.

Tom Dooley, Big John's son, David, and myself went there one Saturday afternoon, baited our lines with cookhouse mutton and flicked them out. Minutes later my line jerked. There before my eyes was an enormous mullet splashing wildly in the water. It shrank a little in landing but was still a fine fish. By that time both Tom Dooley and David were hauling their lines in with mullet on the hooks. For the next twenty minutes it was a frenzy; bait the line, chuck it in and pull out a mullet. The whole settlement would feed on fish.

Then the fish stopped biting, either we had landed the lot or the tide was no longer right. We kept fishing hopefully for the best part of the afternoon; it was warm, we were happy and there would be nothing better to do back at the settlement.

At last we packed up, struggled back to the settlement with our catch and presented the best of them to Jack at the cookhouse kitchen. Jack had been entertaining his whisky bottle. He thanked us profusely. He would prepare a wonderful fish supper for the men.

36: A present of mullet for Jack at San Carlos cookhouse.

Mr Cameron was a keen fly–fisherman and encouraged everyone at KC to take an active interest. When he was fishing he seemed to slip into a world of his own.

He had his rod out at the Cape one weekend and invited us to join him. At the chosen spot, he prepared his fly and explained why he had selected that particular fly and why he felt it was a good place to fish. When all was ready, he became a silent man concentrating on his rod, flicking it just the way he needed to place the fly in the exact spot he wanted until at last a trout rose to it. Mr Cameron played the fish in. When he struck its head on a stone to stun it, a minnow shot from its mouth, a two-in-one catch.

He continued fishing the stretch and presently paused to indicate a small, indeterminate fly above the water. A fish rose, the fly was gone. Mr Cameron allowed himself a single "Ah!" and positioned himself to cast. His fly went to the spot so recently vacated and with his third cast persuaded the fish to rise again. He smiled happily to himself and played it in. No more fish rose but Mr Cameron stayed on, content in his sport. At last he called a halt. His audience was happy to comply.

A species of brown trout had been introduced some years previously to enhance the island stock. Some fine specimens were being caught but an unforeseen consequence was the virtual elimination of the native zebra trout.

Trout fishing became firmly established and one sunny Saturday it was decided to take Redwing up the creek for a family fishing afternoon. The trip was fully booked; adults to fish, children to play along the shore.

The water was calm and the air still. Brook piloted the boat leisurely along the creek, the white dinghy in tow, as ever, in case of accident. The chug-chug of the engine bounced to and fro between the small cliffs lining the shore.

At the chosen bay, Brook dropped anchor. The outboard-motor dinghy became a ferry until everybody was ashore.

The children paddled or went off exploring. Each man chose his spot and prepared his rod. He tied a light metal 'minnow' spinner to his line and was ready. Soon, the shore was lined with fishermen casting and winding in, hopeful that a trout would take their minnow.

The fish seemed disinclined and for ages no one had a bite. Suddenly Tom Dooley gave a suppressed whoop and breathlessly

37: Tom Dooley casts and winds in, hopeful for his first trout.

acclaimed a tug on his line. At last, after weeks of fruitless endeavour, he had enticed a trout to take his minnow.

Tom wound the line in eagerly until the fish surged forward, bidding for freedom. It swam fast and straight, nylon line singing behind it. When it stopped, Tom began steadily winding in once more, waiting for the fish to make its next run. Gradually he played it closer. At last it was in the shallows and could be safely netted. At 3¼ pounds it was no giant but for Tom it was there, the thrill of his first trout. He caught another two smaller fish and was well satisfied with his afternoon.

Brook caught a fine 5½ pound specimen. The rest had to be satisfied with the pleasure of being out fishing.

At six o'clock the children were called away from the picnic fire Fred had lit for them on the beach and Brook ferried everyone back to Redwing. The fishing afternoon was over.

Next morning the wind was up again as so often happened after a calm day. Darwin was due to call at San Carlos to load wool. Fred was to take Redwing round to collect some incoming stores for KC. Although the wind was strong, Fred had no qualms about going as there were no women or children to worry about.

As soon as Redwing was round the settlement bluff, she felt the full force of the wind. She repeatedly buried her bows into waves, throwing sheets of cold salt spray across the men crouched in the lee of the cabin. When she turned at Hospital Point, where the waters always seemed out of order, she rolled and pitched. Each time she crested a wave, her bow see-sawed into the trough, the propeller span in air and the whole boat shuddered. The dinghy dithered behind, one moment falling back until the towline tautened with a resounding crack, the next surging forward and threatening to run aboard .

Darwin approached from Fanning Head, ploughing through the water as if any waves were ripples on a pond. She passed calmly by, leaving an escort of dolphins to accompany Redwing as she bounced about the waves.

By the time Fred turned Redwing at the settlement bay, Darwin was safely anchored there in deep water, with her two barges being lowered over the side. By the time he had made fast at the jetty, the dolphin escort had disappeared.

San Carlos jetty seemed particularly active. Bales of wool were being taken down the jetty railway on the trolley, a familiar enough sight. Less familiar was the sight of three navvies in the settlement rowing boat. Least familiar of all, was the sound of Mr Bonner remonstrating with somebody and looking far from pleased. The swinging ropes of the jetty davits made it clear the boat had only just been launched.

Once Fred and his crew were on the jetty, the picture became clear. Two bales of wool were in the water and the navvies were endeavouring to tow them ashore. The men had allowed the first trolley to run out of control, crash into the wooden buffer block and catapult the front bales into the creek. Small wonder Mr Bonner was upset, especially as the wool was grade AA. Only grade A was of higher value.

The sodden bales were recovered and taken back to the wool-shed to be dried out. The rest of the wool was loaded into the barges and taken out to Darwin. Return trips brought incoming cargo. As soon as the jetty was free of bales, the KC items could be sorted. Among them were boxes of fruit; apples, oranges and bananas. The apples and oranges were sound but once again the bananas proved so over-ripe and oozing they could not be eaten.

High winds and whisky bottles prevented Redwing returning that evening. When Fred went aboard to start the engine next morning he found water in the cabin. During the night's low tide, Redwing must have been aground. It took two hours to pump the water out and locate the leak. The rest of the day was spent repairing the boat.

With the first light of the following morning, Fred was under way. When they arrived back at KC, he had the uncomfortable task of reporting to Mr Cameron and explaining why Redwing had been left in shallow water overnight. Mr Cameron valued Fred as a hard working foreman. Nothing more was said about the incident but Fred was a wise enough man to know how generous a manager his boss was.

THE SCHOOL FLIGHT

Mr Cameron kindly allowed me to take Fandango around the farms so that I had a horse whenever I needed one. This was a great advantage now that Douglas Station was included. As Douglas had more pupils than the combined strength of the San Carloses, it warranted longer visits and meant that the farms could be worked as a circuit instead of a shuttle system. It also meant one less occasion for swimming the horses at KC, a bonus for everyone concerned.

Fandango had an easy-going temperament. He did not mind dawdling on the track or being out all day. The only thing he seemed averse to was hurrying, although he could pick up his heels and go when he wanted to, particularly if there was a stable ahead of him.

Only once did Fandango seem out of sorts and that was a warm, autumn day when I was moving from KC to Douglas. I geared him in the stable, put the bulging maletas across the saddle and led him outside to mount. For some reason, he was uncharacteristically touchy and circled constantly while I hopped around trying to get my foot in the stirrup. I managed at last, gave two quick hops to gain balance and swung up. My leg hooked against the maletas and for a moment I was stuck. Fandango became more disturbed. As I disentangled my foot and flopped into the saddle he attempted to buck. I pulled in hard on the reins. Fandango pulled harder and down went his head. It was instant battle.

There were too many rocks around for me to let myself be thrown so I heaved back on the reins, held on like mad with my legs and hoped he would not buck too long. His first was a real body jerker. It shot me upwards till my legs were taut and my heels clawing at the sheepskin cojinillo. I held on and my backside hit horse again at the crucial impact point for maximum elevation on the second buck. My legs spread wide leaving the stirrups dangling, my left hand gripping the reins tightly. I came down safely just forward of the saddle to straddle Fandango's neck. Two bucks and still mounted, a record. But Fandango's muscles rippled, his body arched and I was away, briefly experiencing free flight as I headed for the ground. I crunched against it and lay there waiting for my hip to inform me whether the pain was a fracture or simply a bruising message about landing speed.

Fandango stopped bucking; he had achieved his purpose. When I had decided I was mobile, I nursed myself to my feet and grasped the cabresto. We returned to the stable where I adjusted the gear and removed several large items from the maletas.

I left the excess luggage at Bill's house, led Fandango out of the stable and tried again. He was his normal self and quietly dawdled me to New House of Glamis and over to Douglas Station.

That school session at Douglas almost coincided with the start of the Darwin Boarding School new term which had begun the previous week. The Beaver schedules had concentrated on transporting scholars back to school. Calm weather meant trouble-free flights but at Douglas they yet again encountered difficulties in ferrying their passengers down to the Moro.

The Rover was at the house in good time to take Jane's brother and sister to the plane but when their mother called them she got no response. The driver put the luggage in the vehicle while she went upstairs to chivvy them. They were not there. Nor were they with friends in the other houses. They seemed to have disappeared completely.

People searched the stables, the wool-shed and the gardens. They called them, said the plane was on its way and the Rover at the gate but all to no avail.

At last the driver could wait no longer and left in case the children had taken it into their heads to begin walking down. He could see no sign of them on the track and when he reached the Moro he had to tell the waiting pilot the passengers could not be found.

The pilot took off and headed for San Carlos to pick up children there. When the plane had passed south over Douglas settlement and was safely away, the two children simply reappeared. They had decided not to return to school and had taken steps to ensure they

38: Jane, Ian and Peter at the Douglas children's dance.

were not on the flight. Their parents chastised them but that was the end of boarding school for Peter and June. They joined Jane and the other boys for the new Douglas session.

Peter and June proved a good pair and the classroom benefited by their presence. They were a great help too when Marj organised a children's games evening to help raise funds for the Girls Life Brigade who were sending some representatives to England for the G.L.B. Golden Jubilee. The children cleared the desks and equipment into as small an area as possible and set out the games. They then spent the evening in competitive teams passing matchboxes along lines of noses, directing blind-folded travellers through a maze of obstacles, puffing through straws to power balloons in relay races and completing a dozen other energy sapping challenges fortified by frequent halts for fruit drinks and specially baked buns. The evening concluded with a special children's dance. It was great fun for them and Marj was able to send a worthwhile cheque to the G.L.B.

The three weeks passed even quicker than usual and I seemed no sooner to have arrived than it was time to move to San Carlos once more. Jock, one of the Douglas navvies, was to be guide via the abandoned house at Third Corral, then over the mountain to the Verde and down to the settlement. It was not so much that Jock was an expert on the track as that it gave him the opportunity for a weekend away from Douglas.

Reaching Third Corral was simple enough. There we stopped and ate the sandwich dinner Marj had prepared for us.

We had hardly started again when a sleet squall hit us head on. It was followed by another two in quick succession and then a real stinker. If we had stopped and turned the horses back-on during the squalls things might have been different. As it was we tried to keep the horses going. They did so but must have been turning imperceptibly to avoid the sleet driving into their faces. When we had a horizon again, it included Mount Usborne and No Man's Land which was positively not our route.

Jock quickly redirected the horses and we made as good time as the ground allowed. The trouble was it was bad ground, getting worse. The nearer we came to the mountains, the softer the ground became. Finally we had to dismount, so far off track that at least we knew we had to turn right.

We turned our back on Mount Usborne and soon found ourselves among bogs that were virtually ponds. It was becoming doubtful whether it was even safe to lead the horses.

We stopped to assess the situation and decided Jock should hold the horses while I went on to see if there was a feasible way through. My boots sank till water was almost over the brim. Prospects were not good.

Jock, being a born optimist, reckoned the horses would make it. He walked cheerfully on. The horses followed and went down to their knees. They seemed to panic a bit and Jock's horse somehow got its foot through Fandango's reins. Both horses lunged forward. Mud flew everywhere. When the commotion finished, Jock's horse was on firmer ground but Fandango was bogged to his belly.

He struggled, settled deeper and stopped struggling. To see a horse in such a position was horrible, to know that it was your doing made it doubly so.

The only thing we could do was attempt to lift the maletas and gear from him. We took off our coats, lay down on them and tried to scoop mud out of the way. It was silly; we were fifteen minutes getting nowhere. Jock took out his knife, cut the straps of the maletas and pulled them clear. We managed to undo the cincha and remove the saddle. At least Fandango was free from gear but of what to do next we had no idea. Fandango remained motionless as if he knew there was no sense in doing anything.

We carried the gear to one side and decided that Jock would have to ride on and get help.

At that point, Fandango made an effort to move, managed to shift a bit and settled back in the bog. We looked on, uncertain whether to be hopeful or resigned. Next he raised his front legs, moved a little, rested a while, lunged forward and was out.

The feeling was not of relief, it was pure ecstasy. We pulled handfuls of grass and did our best to clean the mud off him before leading the horses for the next hour until we were back vaguely where we should be.

Not until the Verde house came into view, making us absolutely certain of our position, did we feel comfortable. The horses could have a rest in shelter while we enjoyed a coffee with the shepherds.

But the Verde was empty and we got no coffee. The horses were given a short rest and then we continued down to reach San Carlos settlement cold, hungry and mighty pleased to be there.

INFERNO

While the number of pupils at Douglas Station increased, the opposite happened at San Carlos.

Just Patrick remained and he spent his days busily engaged in infant department affairs, shopping for empty cereal packets, weighing everything from peat to pencils, matching card labels for his reading book and painting innumerable planes landing on the creek. Even with a 50 per cent cut in pupils the school still needed scrubbing out at the end of the fortnight. That task fell to the teacher.

A bucket of hot water, scrubbing brush and soap passed the time away until supper by which time everything scrubbable had been scrubbed and thoroughly rinsed. For cleanliness it was a masterpiece. Even the window, opened wide to give the wooden floor a chance to dry, sparkled in a way it had not done since George's teaching days. Spring-cleaning made the soul feel good but it was hard on the body. After supper, 'Friday Half Hour' and the current Falkland Radio's play were listened to in the comfort of Ray and Mary's sitting-room.

That night a gale blew up. In the morning there was a knock on the door. Mr Bonner had found the school window torn from its hinges and lying on the green. He was not amused at my lack of thought but as the glass was miraculously intact, the incident was passed over. Four large windows to be glazed in the Falklands would have been of considerable consequence as every pane of glass had to be imported. I apologised and felt considerable relief that it was time to move to KC.

Somewhat subdued, I collected my horse gear and maletas and sought out Billy Gull, the Head of the Bay shepherd, who was providing transport in his jeep. There was a second passenger, a small pig that had arrived from John at Wreck Point via Ajax Bay and the outboard motor dinghy, on its way to Bill at KC. The pig had been bartered for some of Bill's tame geese.

The pig was now a snorting shape inside a thick sack lying reasonably still in the back of the jeep. Billy Gull set off. Although there was plenty of water on the track, it was firm and he lost no time getting up the mountain. At the top a stop was made to check on the pig's condition.

It was a well timed stop. The pig had his head, forelegs and trunk clear of the sack and his back legs were struggling valiantly. A few more minutes and he would have had the run of the island. As it was he could do no more than shriek a prolonged protest as he was unceremoniously bundled back into his sack and securely tied. He gave no more trouble and arrived safely at KC point to cross another creek, this time by rowing boat, and reach his new home.

On the way through the settlement, I called at the Big House to collect my paper mail. Eileen, the governess, had prepared the family a chicken casserole and for no particular reason they extended an invitation for me to share it with them. The aroma was full of promise, so I promptly accepted and indulged in double helpings of chicken casserole capped with tea-berries and cream.

In the evening I went down to the cookhouse. Few people were around that weekend. Pat and his wife, Mali, who had taken over as cook, were away at San Carlos for the weekend as it was Pat's birthday. No outside shepherds were there and the place seemed very quiet.

The living-room was in half darkness. A low fire still glowed in the grate but there was no one to stir the embers or throw another sod on to send sparks up the wide chimney, no one to care that the fire would be out by morning and require tedious relighting; ash to empty, paper, wood and peat chips to arrange and no doubt a carefully distributed potion of paraffin to help the infant flames on their way.

The only noise came from Gyd's room where he and Fred were listening to a record-player and sharing a weekend bottle. They made room for a third person and produced another glass. It was relaxing there, chatting, drinking and sometimes listening to the record on the player. Gyd rustled up a cookhouse Saturday supper; cold mutton, bread and treacle. Drink was already to hand so a kettle was not required. Dusk slowly darkened. Gyd suggested going up to Delhi's. Fred declined as he was comfortably drowsy where he lay crooning a favourite song.

Gyd and I walked through the settlement to Delhi's house and played cards, Chase the Lady till near midnight when the spots on the cards were chasing each other too rapidly for any of us to cope. By the time we went home, the rest of the settlement were buried in sleep.

39: The cookhouse in the evening quiet.

The next morning was a truly glorious one; blue sky, a scattering of cloud and a mild northerly breeze. It seemed set for a warm day.

Bill was up, early as ever, at five o'clock to milk the cows. Brook and his wife were not much later setting out for Race Point to collect diddle-dee berries for making jam and jelly.

During the morning, Arina and I went to feed the pig. Bill had built it a good sty beyond the garden and the pig seemed well settled there. We gave it some food and watched it grunting and snuffling at its breakfast totally absorbed in the pleasures of eating. It finished the lot, checked no morsels were hidden around the corners and stretched out in the shade grunting contentedly to itself.

Clara called across to us. The pig's grunting made it difficult to make out what she was saying. It was something about the settlement because she was pointing that way. Perhaps she had heard somebody across the creek yelling for a boat.

Arina ran up the slope to see what her mother was on about and stood outlined against a rising grey cloud.

"It's the cookhouse. The chimney's on fire."

I hurried to join her. The grey cloud was like a headline. The picture beneath was disturbing. Smoke belched from the far chimney in tight plumes that rose curling and twisting to unfold in a thick blanket above the roof.

People were already hurrying along the valley. Tom, the handyman, and Agnes were already at the cookhouse with Gyd and Fred.

As the others arrived, thick smoke pouring from a skylight exploded into a mass of flame. Almost simultaneously smoke ballooned from the near chimney. Mr Cameron immediately abandoned any idea of trying to save the building and all efforts were concentrated on saving personal belongings.

Men went inside to save what they could. When the door to the ground-floor bedrooms was opened, smoke gushed out defying entry.

40: Thick smoke becomes a mass of flames.

25: Fred cutting peat above Port San Carlos. He has started at first light and the sun is just rising. Peat cutting and warm sun are not a happy combination.

26: Gavin watches Fred dipping sheep to rid them of ticks which debilitate the animal and damage the wool. James and Pat put the sheep in; Fred ducks them with his crook.

27: Delhi and Fred have saved all they can. The Port San Carlos cookhouse must burn.

28: The final fury of the flames. Ladies sort salvaged property; the men move peat clear.

29: The sand trip at Douglas Station. The filled sacks will be rowed out to the Seagull, off loaded at the Moro and transported to the settlement by tractor.

30: Jane faces a fast one. England v Australia on Douglas green. Christine's washing relaxes in the background. Charles passes by unaware of cricket's drama being enacted.

31: Peter sails the Douglas Green. June, Ian and the dogs keep a watchful eye. Strong winds will later bring disaster.

32: The Douglas Greys. June, Ian and Peter mounted for a ride. Terence patiently waiting his turn. Parents were a lot happier when the children were on horses.

Gyd and Fred made one quick dash and had to leave it at that.

Attention was turned to Pat and Mali's room, a single-storey extension on the end of the main building and so far unaffected by smoke. The door was locked. Fred, the biggest man there, put his broad shoulder to the door. It did not budge. He tried again. The whole structure shook but the door stayed firm. The temperature was increasing with alarming rapidity. Delhi left in a hurry.

The crackle of burning wood that had been in the background for the first minutes was now clearer and nearer. The walling was hot to touch and flames were fingering the stairway.

"Gangway. Mind yourselves."

It was Delhi, back with an axe. Two blows and Pat's door was open.

There was the fleeting vision of a peaceful scene; a table with two chairs, ornaments on a dresser, framed pictures on the wall, curtains drawn across the windows. Then the vision vanished as men moved in to save what they could.

Options were closing fast. There was no time to save heavy items or evaluate priorities. Each took what he could, got out quickly and gave it to the ladies forming a chain along the bridge over the stream.

Only two or three entries were possible before the smoke became too much. The room was full of fumes that penetrated the throat and eyes. People put a handkerchief to the mouth, tried to peer through streaming eyes and knew nothing else could be saved. As they left with the last hurriedly grabbed articles, the door was already smouldering.

Outside, the utter hopelessness of the situation was obvious. Fred was detailed to turn the water supply off. The pipe from the reservoir had fractured and water was bubbling into the stream flowing in front of the cookhouse. The background was the blue of the creek. All that water yet none could be utilized.

Tongues of fire appeared along the length of the roof ridge. Flames could be heard gutting the inside.

Gyd thought of the shop at the other end of the building. Again it was a single-storey addition isolated from the intense heat. In it were the food and household stores; sacks of flour and sugar, salt, soap-powders, proprietary medicines, tinned fruit, jams, treacle and boxes of rum, whisky and gin. There was still time to save something if people were quick but Brook, the one man who knew the layout of the store and could direct the salvage efforts, was away.

Once more the axe was put to use and entry gained. The shop was dark at the best of times. Coming in from the bright sun, people simply could not see. A small patch of light by the counter window outlined stacked boxes. Gyd had a reasonable idea of where things were and suggested the best places but even so what was saved was by pure chance. Not until a person reached the door and handed the item to the ladies, could anybody see what it was. Perhaps the man who carried the case of rum had a shrewd idea, the man with the rusted battery clips surely did not.

The rescue operation was short lived. Smoke, already oozing at any gap in the dividing wall, quickly accumulated and without further ado the shop was evacuated.

There was just one more salvage attempt. No flour or sugar had been saved because they were locked in a metal lined cupboard, yet they were the foods most difficult to replace at short notice. Gyd calculated the position of the cupboard and set to with the axe. A small hole was made and Delhi managed to worm his way inside and recover the sugar. The flour was now accessible but the sacks were too bulky for the hole. Gyd began enlarging it but Mr Cameron intervened ordering everybody back to a safe distance. No man was to risk his life for a sack of flour.

People had to stand and watch. The white-painted wall of Pat and Mali's room scorched into flames. The window shattered, spewing another sheet of fire. The tin bath-tub hanging against the outside wall fell as the wood behind it disintegrated.

Boards from the thicker timbers crumbled to feed more air to the blaze within. There came a noise of grating metal as half the roof caved in. Flames and smoke leapt into the air. Reds, oranges, yellows and greys entwined, separated, closed again and were sucked into a towering black smoke cloud. The rest of the roof collapsed in a final crescendo of roaring fire and the whole building seemed to melt into the cloud.

There was no shape left, only a jumble of uncontrolled bonfire on the ground and a high chimney still belching smoke. The cookhouse had gone.

The fire had been fast and furious. It was still not dinner-time, not that any meals were being cooked as all of the ladies were helping to sort salvaged property. A cup of tea was the greatest need and there were plenty of volunteers to make it. Fred pointed out that the water supply was cut off and he wistfully eyed the case of rum that had been saved. Mr Cameron solved the dilemma by distributing another salvaged item, a case of strawberry fizz. It served well enough.

Nobody had been badly hurt but Gyd had cuts on his arm and back and Tom had sustained a deep cut on his wrist. Although the blood had soaked through the bandage, Tom declared it was 'nothing much' and carried on shifting smouldering peat sods that threatened to ignite the complete cookhouse supply. There was no need to lose the peat as well.

Gradually the bonfire flames died down. The old cookhouse was represented by a twisted heap of iron bedsteads, distorted corrugated roofing and one tall chimney. In the afternoon everything was thoroughly doused and the chimney pulled down. By evening next day the site had been cleared and the only reminders of the disaster were the scorched ground, a new view of the creek and a group of homeless men.

Arrangements were quickly made for the settlement families to house the homeless until sufficient beds and furniture could be collected and installed in the dance hall which would become the temporary cookhouse.

When Pat and Mali returned from their weekend celebrations they had the shock of discovering that their home had been destroyed.

"Fox Bay Calling Stanley"

Mr Cameron ordered a new cookhouse, specially designed in prefabricated sections, to be shipped out as soon as possible. Meanwhile, the single men had tedious months of living in the dance hall.

When the new cookhouse arrived, KC became a full-time building site. The settlement valley was always prone to mud in wet weather. Now it became a veritable mud-bath as tractors brought more sand from the sand bay for the cement mixer and rocks from the mountain to fill in some of the worst holes left where tractors or trailers had been bogged.

Work went ahead at full speed; motivation had never been so good. The foundations were down in no time and the prefabricated sections in position as soon as the concrete allowed. Once the central chimney was complete, the men would be able to count the days to moving into their new accommodation.

Their present living conditions were certainly basic. The main dance hall was part dining area and part dormitory, furnished with a varied collection of beds, each with one of the steel-framed hall chairs beside it and an assortment of boxes or borrowed cases for personal belongings. The school room had become a bed-sitter for Pat and Mali.

Mali cooked in the little kitchen where the old stove had been replaced by a Rayburn cooker with a back-boiler for heating water. As there was no bath, the settlement families made theirs available and everybody coped.

The men were soon to count their blessings at being in good health, albeit a little short of comforts, when the early morning R/T schedules were interrupted by a call from a West Falkland farm.

"Hello, Stanley. Hello, Stanley. This is Fox Bay West calling Stanley. Are you receiving me please? Over."

"Hello, Fox Bay. Stanley receiving you. Over."

"Syd, I have an urgent medical call from the doctor. He has a patient here, a shepherd in need of immediate hospital attention, a stretcher case. Can you arrange with the air service and hospital please, and have transport laid on from the hangar? Over."

"Yes. I've got all that. What's your weather?"

"Winds gusting, Syd, and the first snow squalls reaching us. The doctor would like to talk with the hospital if you could arrange it. Over."

"I've got that. I'll call you back as soon as I've contacted people. Out."

Within minutes he was back on the air.

"Hello, Fox Bay. The plane will be on its way as soon as they've made the cabin adjustments for the stretcher. Doctor Brown will be down from the hospital in about ten minutes. Over."

"Thank you, Syd. Snow's pretty bad here now. I reckon we'll be closed down within the hour. Over."

"Yes, Fox Bay, I'll pass that on. They've got blizzard conditions from New Island to Hill Cove. Flights there are cancelled but they are confident about reaching you. I'll let you know when they've taken off. Over."

"Thank you, Syd. I'll be standing by. Out."

When the doctor came on the air it transpired that the patient had acute appendicitis which was not going to wait for the weather to clear. If the patient could not be flown in, the doctor would have to operate at Fox Bay. It was real life drama.

The air service mechanics quickly made the necessary adjustments and within half an hour Stanley was able to inform Fox Bay that the plane was on its way.

The first snow squalls were now hitting East Falkland settlements. People knew the plane would not normally fly in such conditions and many re-tuned their radio to the plane's frequency to listen to messages between the pilot and Stanley Flight Control.

They heard nothing until the plane passed Darwin Camp and was crossing the Falkland Sound. Then came the voice of Jim Kerr, the Air Service's senior pilot, contacting control, "Approaching Fox Bay.

Visibility poor. Water choppy. Making approach run."

"Roger."

Before long, the transfer of the patient to the plane was being reported.

In twenty minutes they had him safely aboard and were waiting for a squall to finish.

It was a prolonged squall and a further half-hour passed before the weather cleared and Jim Kerr announced he was taking off.

Stanley's reply was discouraging, "Met. Office reports continuous snow. Visibility here is nil. Darwin is clear. I suggest you land there."

"Patient is in a bad way. Am heading for Stanley. Please have road transport standing by."

There was another long period of silence. To people clustered round their radios the wait seemed interminable and the snow swirling past the windows appeared to be worse each second. Somewhere in it was the plane with its pilot and a very sick man. Every minute dragged like an hour. Twenty-five minutes passed, half-an-hour and still no word. At last people unwillingly accepted that an accident could have happened. They discussed the hazards; Mount Usborne, engine failure, icing, lost directions. Something had happened, but what?

Thirty-five minutes, Jim Kerr surely never went that time without making contact. There must have been time for him to reach Stanley. With each dragging minute, people's doubts became firmer fears. The plane was in trouble.

At last there was a crackle on the radio and Jim Kerr's faint voice, "Approaching Stanley now. Am coming straight in."

The tension eased. Jim Kerr had got his plane safely through, as reliable as ever, just like everybody thought he would do. Only what a snow storm to do it in.

Radios were tuned back to 4.5 megs and soon Stanley was heard contacting Fox Bay, "Plane landed a few minutes ago and the patient is on his way to hospital. The weather's right in again. They were lucky."

"That's great news, Syd. Please pass on our thanks to the hangar."

"Yes, I'll do that. We'll let you know how he is tomorrow morning. Out."

The next morning's message was encouraging. The offending appendix had been removed and the patient was as well as could be expected.

The disruption to air services continued for several days. It almost spoilt the big occasion that Ginger, the new shepherd at KC, and his youngest daughter, Betty, had been anticipating for months, the marriage of one of Ginger's older daughters in Stanley Cathedral.

The ceremony would take place the coming Saturday afternoon and Betty was to be a bridesmaid. High winds and flight cancellations on Thursday and Friday augured bitter disappointment but Saturday kept calm, the pilot made a special flight to KC and the day was saved.

That afternoon the sun shone on the bride. All of her family were there to share her happiness and to give the pair a great send off at the wedding celebrations in the town hall.

The happy events of the weekend were followed on the Tuesday by the discovery of a body in the public toilets. It was identified as that of Bun, a one-time cook at Douglas Station and he had apparently lain there all night. There was no question of foul play, only a tragic case of the ultimate consequences of drink. Bun had reached the stage where people had to lock up the methylated spirit for their Tilley lamps or he would be liable to drink it. He had been black listed many times and was banned from the Stanley bars but his craving led him to try any substitute until finally he and his crony had taken something that caused almost instant poisoning and what must have been a horribly painful and lonely death.

They managed to find his drinking partner. They rushed him to hospital but they could not save him.

Two dead. The news rocked the drinkers. At Douglas Station, Bert was visibly shaken. Bert had been a mate of Bun's at the cookhouse where they had enjoyed years of weekend inebriety together. Bert still loved his Saturday bottle and would not be without it but he had never allowed it to prevent him turning-to on Monday morning even if he was more 'away' than 'there'. The Stanley deaths changed everything. Bert renounced the bottle. His friendly weekend drunkenness became a rather touchy sobriety.

CURVE-HORNED AND MUD KNOTTED

Bert's pledge to sobriety was soon to be tested. It was just a week to the Douglas Station two-nighter dance and they had decided to follow the San Carlos lead in having steer riding. The drink would flow. Bert would need to be at his strongest to keep clear of it.

Meanwhile, Bert had plenty to do to keep him busy and out of temptation's way.

Mr Greenshields, the owner of Douglas Station, was out on a visit from his Welsh farmlands. He had decided that the dance hall should be updated with central heating in readiness for the two-nighter. Somehow the necessary equipment was assembled. Bert and his fellow navvies worked with a will but the time schedule was tight.

Everybody was fully in favour of the central heating. It would mean warm whist drives, warm films and warm dances but the greatest beneficiary would be the school.

The Douglas School term had just begun. Because the main dance hall was a mass of loose pipes and radiators, school was restricted to the refreshment room in the corner. Terence declared it was the freshest feeling refreshment room he had ever been in and the rest of us agreed. Three Tilley heaters were lit to make life bearable and they soon created a cosy fug in the room.

Morning lessons were as practical as possible. Peter and June were at the sink trying to work out the volume of a penguin egg kindly provided by their mother with strict instructions that it was to be returned intact. Terence and Ian had a tape measure and were immersed in higher maths trying to calculate the length of piping there would be in the hall by the time the central heating was finished. Jane was busy with her new reading book.

They all had one ear cocked for the sound of the Beaver. A mail drop was being made that day and the children had been promised a minute or two off to watch it. At least half their attention had to be for the plane because the pilot would fly straight over, drop the mail and be away to the next place.

It was Terence who heard the plane. A fire-drill could not have matched the exodus. In no time they were at their allotted 'safe' positions under the eaves of the hall as the Beaver rapidly drew near and swept overhead.

The pilot could be seen at the window with the mail bag. He released it and waved. The bag entangled in the float-struts and continued with the plane.

"Hey! The mail!"

"Come back!"

"You've got it stuck!"

The children shouted their protests into the roaring engine as the plane disappeared beyond the hall. They chased round the corner gesticulating wildly.

House doors quickly opened and the Douglas womenfolk assembled on the green to discuss the matter. The engine note had already changed and the plane was turning slowly round towards the settlement. The pilot clearly knew he had not made a successful drop.

He levelled the plane once more and came back. He flew straight as a die over the houses and banked steeply above the green to dislodge the bag. Nothing fell and the plane was out above the creek.

Hopes for release changed abruptly as the plane seemed to linger over the water while the pilot made another careful turn. After long seconds the plane was once more safely above land coming in over the wool-shed, zooming over the green and banking sharply again.

The mail bag plummeted to earth, the pilot waggled his wings and everyone cheered. The children waved to the fast receding plane and returned to school while the foreman set off to locate the mail somewhere beyond the cowman's house.

Douglas Station families were hardly surprised at the near loss of the mail. There seemed to be a jinx at large affecting shepherds and navvies alike.

The shepherds had the most to put up with when they gathered the Mountains Camp flock ready for dipping. Mist and low cloud had hung over the mountains making it very difficult to locate the sheep. Consequently, the men were away more days than usual, cooped up each night in Docherty's Shanty, a small hut completely devoid of comfort or sanitation.

When at last the flock had been driven back to the settlement, it turned out there were 600 less sheep for dipping than had been sheared. Losses were never that high. There were hundreds of undipped sheep still at large to spread the parasitic lice and ticks that weakened the animals and stained the wool.

The manager sent the shepherds to gather the mountains a second time. They still failed to find enough sheep. Even when sheep were sighted, it did not mean they could be brought in. The sheep invariably sighted the shepherd first and if they moved in among the stone runs they blended with the rocks. The shepherd could well call his dogs away to another group which as far as he knew were the first sheep showing again.

Misfortune dogged the navvies when they took Seagull out for a load of sand. They set off in early morning darkness at six o'clock on the ebb tide and spent a freezing day at an island filling sandbags, humping them into the rowing boat, rowing them to Seagull anchored outside the thick kelp fronds and hoisting them aboard. They were making good time home on the incoming tide when an oil pipe fractured obliging them to drop anchor to effect repairs. They limped the rest of the way back to the Moro, humped the sand bags from Seagull onto the trailers, moored Seagull, climbed aboard the tractors and set off for the settlement. On the way, one of the tractors broke down.

In fact the only event that seemed to run smoothly was the movement of the beef quota going to Stanley. That was a straight hand over in Douglas Corral by the Salvador drovers, who had brought the beef, to the Teal Inlet men responsible for the next part of the drive. It had not involved Douglas men at all.

It was small wonder that no one had high hopes for the completion of the central heating on time. Everyone concerned worked at full stretch as Douglas was hoping for plenty of visitors. While the ladies sweated in their kitchens baking bread and buns, the men froze in the hall cutting and joining pipes and radiators.

By Friday evening, there were plenty of visitors and ample food but the central heating was still a pipe or two short. The hall had to be warmed by Tilley lamps. Not that the dancers suffered by it; six hours' dancing made some of them comfortably warm and others unbearably hot. When the dance ended, they stepped outside to go home and had the surprise of slipping in snow.

They woke later to find a beautiful snowscape from the green to the distant mountains where a blanket of ominous cloud posed a threat to the day's steer riding. Fortunately a breeze cleared the cloud and the sun found enough warmth to thaw the snow.

The cattle had been herded down from the mountains earlier in the week and looked more than half wild with wide curved horns and long unkempt winter coats curled and mud knotted. Now they were driven from the horse paddock into the corral. Spectators and contestants gathered to inspect them, debating which beasts would give the liveliest rides. An eventful day was anticipated.

The assistants assembled in the corral. One of them prepared a lasso. The first bullock was looped and driven into the banding-race but before the bars could be slid across, it turned and ran back to the herd which huddled together, milling around uncertainly and churning the centre of the corral to mud.

Men grabbed hold of the lasso. Once more the animal was driven in and once more it was out before the bars could be secured. The catchers went into their own huddle to decide on a strategy. They adjourned to the stable.

After lengthy discussions a rider emerged. The gate from the corral to the horse-paddock was opened and the cattle were driven out. There were moans of disbelief from the thoroughly chilled spectators and a horrified roar from the stable. The rider had well and truly blundered.

Off went riders in pursuit. Assistants roped boards together to narrow the banding-pen and spectators cleared off home for coffee.

Before too long the cattle were back at a smart pace with Douglas dogs snapping at their heels. They splashed into the mud of the corral and stood eyeing the reassembling spectators. A lasso snaked through the air; a bullock bellowed and bucked and more mud flew around.

This time there was no snag. The bullock was manoeuvred to the banding-race, the belly bands were put in place and Hamish, the honoured first rider, lowered himself onto the animal's shoulders. He gripped the bands and announced he was ready.

The gate swung open and out cavorted the bullock. It bucked and twisted, head down bellowing protests with wide-spread horns almost furrowing the ground but Hamish's gaunt figure swayed to the bullock's jumps and refused to be dislodged. The bullock bucked to a standstill. Hamish slid from its back and it straightway lowered its head and crashed through the fencing to the mud and companionship of the corral.

The third animal, a black beast with the usual spread of horns, was the chance for me to improve my buck-jumping abilities. I lowered myself onto the bullock's back, seized the belly-band so tight my knuckles stood out white, set my weight back and yelled, "Let her go!"

The gate opened and I was in a twisting, thumping momentum of sweat-tight knees, with wrists clamped and wrenched and a jerking, pummelled stomach. My eyes focused on huge sharp prongs of horn round snorted spouts of steamy breath till a sudden greenness crunched through my body and everything was still.

"Five seconds," called a voice as the bullock went away. Five seconds?

After a couple more riders had been thrown, a halt was made for dinner. The hour's break seemed to do nothing good for the animals, some of which seemed decidedly ill-tempered, especially one black thick-set beast with down-curved horns that went for anyone rash enough to cross its path. One of the catchers managed to lasso it but before a turn could be made with the rope, the animal rounded on the men and sent them scurrying through the mud for safety.

Again and again they tried to drive it to the banding-pen but each time it turned on them till Gerald was trapped and the bullock pinned him against the fence. Luckily the animal turned and skulked to a corner leaving Gerald unnerved and shaken but thankfully unhurt.

After that, a horseman was called in. The free end of the lasso was made fast to the horse's gear and the bullock was pulled unwillingly to the pen. Bands were put on and a rider seated himself astride it.

When the gate opened, the bullock bucked out, deposited its rider on the green and cleared off out of it, belly bands and all. He later turned up again at the gate on the horse paddock side of the corral, having broken through two fences to get there. The gate was opened for him and he re-entered for all the world like a conquering hero.

A red, hornless bullock almost outmatched him. As the lasso settled over it, it lowered its head and pawed the ground in threatening manner. Stalwart men scattered but one broad-shouldered man stood firm, Mr Greenshields.

He closed smartly on the animal, leant his frame across its neck, seized its head in both hands and matched his muscle and guile against the animal's. Slowly it was forced to slither through the mud towards the pen with Mr Greenshields leaning almost horizontally as he searched for footholds.

Somebody pulled back the pen gate, another man moved to help and the bullock made a last desperate struggle in the quagmire.

There was a flurry of feet, a scurry of figures and Mr Greenshields flat in the mud with the bullock on top of him. The animal came to its feet in a sheet of grey-brown ooze and made for the herd, trailing the loose lasso. The rope jerked tight round Mr Greenshield's leg and flipped him helplessly over to be trawled face down behind the bellowing bullock.

For an instant people numbed, then men were dashing forward. The animal was halted and the rope was slackened. To everyone's surprise, the mud-clad figure struggled to his feet, cleared a portion of mud from his face and gave a loud chuckle. Undaunted he set at the bullock again, this time with ample assistance, and got it into the pen.

It was the last incident of the day. Riders came and riders went until as dusk fell the final animal threw its man to make an end of Douglas Station steer riding. The corral gate opened and the herd moved out into the horse-paddock to trot off into the setting sun in true Western style.

FISH FULL FRIED

It was high summer. Three years had almost passed. The Douglas Station school session would be my last, an extended one of a full four weeks with a school roll actually reaching double figures. The usual six children were joined by Sharon, the cousin of Terence and Ian, Robin and Gerard on extended holiday from Stanley and Ramond, a Chilean boy of great determination, who refused to accept that he could have any inkling of the English language.

It was a good session. Peter was practical minded and was for ever constructing things with wood. It was Peter who inspired the sectioned vaulting horse fashioned from wood oddments supplied by his Uncle Darwin. When the last tack had been hammered in to fasten the padding firmly down, the horse was paraded onto the green and vaulting commenced.

41: Peter tries out his vaulting horse.

The vaulting horse attracted them all and it was not long before there were adjustable high-jump stands and hurdles. Peter's long spear became a javelin, a biscuit-tin lid became a discus, the green provided both a running track and, with a little spade work, a jumping pit and the Douglas Station Athletics Club was in being. The meetings were keenly contested and finally had people practising 'miles' before breakfast.

42: June proves champion high jumper.

The warm evenings made cricket a worthwhile venture. Soon England and Australia were fighting for the ashes. Bats were prime-quality packing case, shaped and sanded to the cricketer's personal requirements. The wickets were two school chairs.

Fielding reached an extremely high standard when the settlement dogs were around but they upset the flow of the game. Without them, there were runs a plenty and everyone was far happier. The batsman did not feel his best hit was thwarted, the fielder was not constantly harried and the bowler did not have to worry about bowling with a saliva coated ball.

Matches were open ended and stumps were seldom drawn until a hard-hit ball in the gloaming resulted in a dozen or more runs being

43: Evening shadows lengthen as Terence hits out. Sadly, Brian, to left of picture, lost his life trying to save his younger brother in a fishing accident at Stanley harbour.

completed without the ball being found. Then the wickets were folded and taken back to the hall and the children retired to their homes.

They enjoyed both athletics and cricket but neither seriously challenged horse riding or fishing. When the children set off for a ride on the Douglas Greys they were really in their element. As there were three Douglas Greys to five riders it was a case of turn and turn about but the children were quite content. The adults were a lot happier too. Riding had far more purpose to it. Their children were the future islanders and the skills of horsemanship far outweighed those of cricket.

Marj and Owen took the boys on fishing trips to a favoured spot in Teal Inlet Camp which sometimes resulted in a fine trout and sometimes in nothing.

The children had their eyes on the shoals of small fish closer to home in the narrow creek beside the settlement. When the light was right, the myriad flickers of silver in the shallow water showed the harvest that was ready for gathering. It just needed a little initiative to determine how it should be done.

Fishing became a highly organised team undertaking. Peter decided a large net was required. Uncle Darwin was again called upon to provide the raw materials, hessian bagging that would normally cover the wool bales and strong thread for sewing it. First they fashioned a keep net and then they sewed lengths of bagging on until they had extended it to some four metres wide with towing ropes at the two leading corners and lumps of metal to keep the bottom part weighted down.

They had the net. All they had to do now was trawl it through the creek. Peter explained how it was to be done. First priority was to get rid of shoes and socks and roll trousers above the knees. Power for the trawl would be children wading.

June took the nearside rope and Peter dragged the other end into the creek. The younger ones, armed with sticks, went a hundred metres along the bank and spread out across the water. Fishing could begin.

The younger ones slowly waded towards the net beating the water to drive the fish forward. When they met together, Peter and June trawled the net towards shore. It was heavy and as much as they could do to shift but with the rope round their shoulders and backs well bent they managed to get under way.

As they approached land, the spare beaters declared they could see hundreds of fish leaping around. The net was beached and when the folds were turned back there was a unified shout of triumph as fish flicked in the muddy sediment. The fishermen gathered their catch into a bucket, stood it on the bank and began another sweep.

Results were not so exciting and the coldness of the water was beginning to tell. The skipper decided the tear in the net would not survive a third trawl and the crew declared themselves ready to sign off for dinner.

Almost a hundred fish had been caught, some as long as a fisherman's finger. An invitation to supper at Peter's house was extended to the crew and to Uncle Darwin who had made the whole thing possible.

During the afternoon the children went tea-berrying and in the evening they feasted on fish (full fried with head and tail) followed by a dessert of tea-berries. Satisfaction was complete.

Peter's most ambitious venture was to convert his go-cart to a land-yacht. It was a project of the utmost importance for which everything else was set aside. First he researched the school library for advice on sails. It did not take him long. What reference books there were came from private donations and most of that from the teacher, perhaps a 'thank you' for the minimal lodging-rate paid to the parents and the generous facilities provided by them.

Peter drew his plans and searched around the wood store until he found suitable timber for a mast and boom. Hessian bagging came into its own again as sail-cloth and he made himself a triangular sail.

The completed yacht was wheeled out to the green. There was a fair breeze blowing and the children looked on expectantly as Peter hoisted his sail. It ran up to the masthead well and he angled the boom to catch the maximum wind but the ship held fast and the intrepid sailor got nowhere. Peter decided a simpler sail might catch the wind better.

He made the boom into a cross-yard and enlarged the sail to a rectangle so that his craft became a 'square-rigger'. He cut more bagging twine, sorted out the rigging and discovered the best way to hoist and make-fast his sail.

Finally satisfied, he pushed his craft clear of the building to catch the wind and began hoisting the sail. It went up smoothly two-thirds of the way when the wind whipped it round enveloping Peter and defeating all his efforts to disentangle himself. Terence and Ian salvaged him and they considered the next move.

They towed the craft to the lee of the dance-hall where the green sloped gently down towards the houses and prepared for another launch. Peter hoisted his sail, tied the rigging securely and sat waiting.

Terence pushed him clear of the hall, the wind filled the sail and the yacht was on its way.

Peter sailed slowly across the green with a look of utter contentment on his face.

The dogs caught sight of the new craft and came snapping round it like sharks. Peter was oblivious to them, he was sailing.

The better the wind, the better the voyage. It did not need much above a breeze to make passengers a possibility. Pleasure trips from the hall to Peter's house became the order of the day.

44: Jane enjoys a cruise across the green.

Normally the yacht was accompanied by children walking or part trotting but the day came when the wind was half a gale and the children decided they would need their bikes if they were not to be left behind. Conditions seemed right for a voyage from the stable on the far side of the green. It would be a solo run. No passenger; just Peter and the yacht, a chance to really sail.

They assembled at the stable. The sail was raised, bicycles were mounted, and Peter was pushed clear.

As the wind caught the sail, the yacht moved off. For a few moments the cyclists kept pace but once clear of the stable the elements took command. The yacht shot away and was soon being blown across the grass at a speed far greater than Peter could manage.

When he pulled on a steering rope the whole craft tilted on two wheels threatening to overturn. Only one course was open to him, get the sail down or be wrecked.

Peter kept his nerve and struggled to lower the sail but he had secured it with a granny knot that simply would not budge. The yacht was whisked past the dance hall to the slope leading down from it. On the horizon were the settlement houses like a ragged line of rocks. He looked doomed to a head-on collision with the wooden palings of Christine's garden fence.

With a last desperate effort, he heaved on the steering rope. The yacht came half round, tilted and capsized, spread-eagling Peter on the green. For a moment or two he lay there surveying the scene. The yacht was hard against the fence, the mast snapped in two and beyond repair. But what did it matter? He had sailed Douglas Green. Now it was time for something different.

AND NOW

For me it was time to leave the Falklands. I had arrived in sunshine but was to leave in the driving rain of a dreary Monday evening. At 9.00 p.m. R.M.S. Darwin hooted her monthly farewell and moved slowly out from Port Stanley.

By morning she was alone in the rolling South Atlantic. Somewhere behind the horizon were the Falkland Islands; peat smoke above the chimneys, R/Ts keeping everyone in touch with everyone else's news, the Beavers revving across the creek, sheep everywhere but nowhere to be seen, a Falkland wind blowing through the white grassed hills, mutton in the meat-house and a full day's work ahead to keep the wool-bins full.

Darwin steamed on to Montevideo. There her passengers joined a ship for Europe and Darwin set sail for Stanley again.

45: R.M.S.Darwin at Montevideo alongside R.M.S. Arlanza, the liner for Europe.

Time slipped quietly away; days into weeks, weeks into months and months suddenly into years. Letters brought news of children growing, babies born and new developments in Town and Camp. The Post Office issued new stamps. The Royal Marines boosted rugby among their official activities.

On the farms, Land Rovers came into greater use. At KC, Keith took the crawler-tractor out making tracks to each lamb-marking pen to make them more accessible for vehicles. He and some of the younger shepherds experimented with motor bikes as transport around their flocks. The idea of motorized shepherding gradually spread, although in areas like Wreck Point that were strewn with rocks, the horse remained supreme.

By 1978 the 1800 islanders had a total of 984 motor vehicles for which there were six miles of macadamized roads in and around Stanley. Elsewhere it was still mud tracks or open grassland. An expert was brought in to give advice on constructing a proper road network.

The islanders were becoming accustomed to receiving teams of British experts whose advice, profound or straightforward, was well enough formulated but not always so readily translatable to practical application.

An economic survey team included experts on fisheries, oil and wool. Tourism was mooted as a major project with the island wildlife the main attraction. Grass experts experimented to find ways to improve the pasture and increase the yield from the vast area given over to sheep.

A large tract of land north of Stanley was split into smaller units and islanders were invited to apply for them. Tony from Cape Dolphin and Peter from Douglas Station were both successful. They were now skilled men willing to put in the hours of hard work necessary to make a success of their opportunities.

Hardly had they started when the all-important wool prices fell, threatening ruin to the small farmer. For a while the outlook was grim but neither man lost his resolve. Both farms survived the difficult period to become firmly established.

Bill and Clara eventually moved from KC to Newhouse of Glamis, the isolated house midway along the riding track to Douglas Station. Stan and Muzzie left Cape Dolphin and moved to KC to look after the Big House. Owen and Marj gave up Camp life at Douglas for a position with Stanley Post Office. Ray and Mary also moved into Stanley from JB.

Managers found it difficult to fill places on the farms.

British politicians talked of greater co-operation with the Argentine, of developing closer links. The theme was steadily pursued. British aid funds enabled a project for a permanent air-strip to go ahead. The Argentine government gave its full backing and a site was selected east of Stanley. It was long, slow work but eventually a runway was completed to a length enabling a regular link to be established with the Argentine at Comodoro Rivadavia.

Air travel was now possible anywhere. All the islander had to do was fly to Comodoro Rivadavia and apply for a 'white-card' permitting travel through Argentina to Buenos Aires where all the world was his oyster; with one catch.

Patrick discovered that catch on his first trip from the islands. When he produced his white-card at Buenos Aires, the airport official waved it to one side informing him that as he was from Islas Malvinas, he had been living in the Argentine all his life. Patrick's reply was politely abrupt, "Oh no I haven't. I'm a Falkland Islander." He was waved on with a wry smile.

For the administration in Stanley it was a dilemma. Commercial co-operation with the South American continent could be beneficial but it had to be carefully monitored or the islands would find themselves too dependent on neighbouring countries. Already the Falkland Islands Company had sold R.M.S. Darwin; the main sea link had gone.

If the islanders wanted to keep their identity, they had to show they were still a viable entity ready to stand out against political dealing, against being dictated to by either Britain or the Argentine.

They did stand out. They sent their elected representatives to the special committee on colonialism at the United Nations. There they stated their position. They were Falkland Islanders. They held a close association with Britain and chose to maintain it. They were utterly opposed to any political ties with South American countries and would not be subjugated by them. It was simple, basic and patently clear. Their homes were to remain their homes; Home, The Falkland Islands, South Atlantic.

Their warnings and forebodings were quietly dismissed by successive U.K. governments over-burdened with crucial issues that left little or no room for the far flung Falklands.

Then came 2nd April 1982. A night of alarming gunfire, a morning of enemy soldiers patrolling with rifles poised; the Argies in Town. The dormant threat had become inescapable fact; the islanders were trapped and events were out of their hands.

Some families moved to relatives on the farms. Some had to sweat it out in Stanley. Many people, both in Town and in Camp, had far more to contend with than the outside world could know. Communications faded and went.

Not until the British forces landed could people relate what had really been going on. When the troops went ashore at Port San Carlos, Stan and Muzzie were able to write to their son in the U.K. and to me and my family,

Port San Carlos
26 May 1982.

Dear Frances, Ted and children,
Well as you must know by now we are right in the middle of a war. I hope soon over too. I'm writing this as we are told we would get a mail away today. We are all well here at KC but lord only knows what could happen by tonight. It is not light yet. They started the first raid at seven o'clock yesterday. One broke the glass in the front porch. We've got a big hole dug at the office door and go in it for shelter. There are holes dug everywhere. The first we knew the British were here was when they woke us up at one in the morning – they were shelling Fanning Head as the Argies had a lot of men up there. When we got up in the morning the harbour was full of ships and men coming up from the Sand Bay by the

thousands. There were about forty Argies camped in the dance hall and they made off down towards the Knob, Cerro Montevideo. They left everything they had. The troops have not gone to look for the Argies, they say they won't live long with no food or shelter. Maybe one of their own choppers has picked them up. We are still having nice weather. The troops are hoping for fog so we don't get so many raids.

Well I'd better stop as this goes out with the forces mail today, so I'll say love to all and hope not too long before this is all over,

Muzzie, Stan.

The next month a letter came from Bill and Clara at Douglas Station. They had temporarily left their isolated home at Newhouse of Glamis and moved into the settlement.

Douglas Station

Dear Ted, Frances and family,

Hope all is well with you. We have had our dear older folks with us for the past three months. My mum, her sister and husband and Bill's mum and her husband. All are over seventy. We've also had the Argentines. The first lot took our two metre sets away to stop us making contact with anyone. The next lot took all the radios they could find saying we were not to listen to the B.B.C. A week after that lot left I went out to our home at Newhouse to collect some things and found the place wrecked. A pool of blood was in the hall, bullet holes everywhere and empty shells among the appalling mess and ruin. Two dead hens lay on the kitchen table tied by the ankles and two more lay in the bath – this made me furious. Ash was in the bath, plastic bins were burnt with it, ash was in cardboard boxes and all over the floor. You couldn't see the floor in any rooms – urine, sheep bones and heads, furniture upturned, materials thrown around, cases broken into and scattered, curtains ripped, bed piled over an open window. The lid was off the ceiling loft so I beat a hasty retreat in case

*the Argies were still about. But the worst time we had was
after we heard the B.B.C. say 41 Argentines had gone off into
the Camp from Port San Carlos when the British landed there
and no one knew where the Argies had gone to. We knew they
would try to reach Stanley and day after day we waited
expecting them to appear here. The waiting was awful. We
couldn't contact Teal Inlet because the Argies had outposts
each side of us – and the ones on Chata Hill had our phone
bugged. There was nowhere we could go so we just had to stay
and wait. Then early one Sunday morning they were here –
wearing our hats, jackets and coats, and carrying our cases
stolen from our home at Newhouse! They must have lived
several days out there. My mother had not yet got up and the
soldiers went up to the bedroom and ordered her out. It was a
very frosty morning but we were taken outside and had to stay
there until everyone was collected. They herded us together
and put us in the cold dance-hall where we were kept four
days while they lived in the warmth of our houses, ate up all
our precious food, and looted again. Two women were allowed
once a day under armed guard to cook a hot meal. A guard
was kept at the hall day and night. Every night they came into
the hall to count us and the same first thing in the morning.
They were young, scared, fleeing and dangerous. No one
opposed them in any way. At last they left in four of their
helicopters. Two days later the British troops arrived. It was a
real happy and grand sight to see all those hundreds of men
walking in. We cheered and hugged them but felt for them too.
Now we are rejoicing when we hear of the troops arriving
safely home in U.K. It's sad so many were killed.*
 Very much love to you all,
  Clara, Bill and family.

Out at Horseshoe Bay, Peter and his wife, Margie, had not been so
personally affected but they were still very much involved. The islands
were too small for it to be otherwise. They wrote of their experiences:

"Gosh what shambles around! Ourselves, we only had one visit by the Argies and that was enough. They came in a chopper armed to the teeth and asking all the questions under the sun. One chap was a right one – he looked a right killer, seemed to try and make fun of everything we said. Imagine it, they even asked if we had grenades in the house. They didn't go into our home but my sister's house in Stanley had been looted and the mud is six inches deep on her carpets and the windows are smashed. Quite a lot of people have the same experience.

We had lots of Harriers flying low too – we could see the pilot easily. One day we got a terrible scare, seven Argie Sky Hawks were on the run out our way. We saw one shot down over Teal Inlet and another went over the house very low, smoke pouring out of it. We all ducked as it made a terrible noise. Our main fear was night time as the Argies started dropping bombs anywhere. Green Patch came close to being hit twice. Those bombs were meant for Mount Kent area and landed in the water about 100 yards off the houses. The explosions were so loud and sometimes kept on all night – we don't want to go through that again.

The Argies had lookouts on most high hills so we had them on our boundary. I hope they didn't put mines down out there. The people at the Murrel had lots of their animals with crippled legs swinging in an awful state. Oh I hope the Brits keep the place after the way they got it back otherwise all those poor men died for nothing. We'll certainly stay if it remains British and they keep the Argies out of our land.

The place will never be the same. We realise we can't live like we did in the past and look forward to the new challenges. Our shearing season is drawing near. We have a fine bunch of sheep this year, all big and healthy-looking so here's to a bumper wool clip. Our last one was good and our wool report excellent. We pressed 64 bales of about 300 kilos each. Nineteen thousand kilos of prime Falkland wool. So here's to the future."

And now that future is twenty years on. Roads link the settlements. Two days riding has become a couple of hours' drive. Voices on a phone with the U.K. are clearer than those on the line between farm houses ever were. Personal computers on the Web, satellite T.V. and eager tourists arriving by ship and plane, shrink time and distance.

It is a future very different from the past. The islanders on their smaller farms still sweat to keep the wool bins full and have all the difficulties and delights of the shepherd's year but the continuing depressed wool prices mean scant return for the farmer's hard graft.

Peter and Margie stayed on at Horseshoe Bay and their children have had the farm as their home. Tony's family has grown up at the nearby Estancia. Gerald took on Wreck Point where he still keeps up the traditional way of shepherding by horseback. Terence has another of the San Carlos farms. Ian achieved a boyhood ambition of becoming an airline pilot. Patrick has Bill and Clara's KC house, converted as tourist accommodation. Arina is on Pebble Island where they have about a hundred pigs; some difference from the little piglet she was feeding the day the KC cookhouse went up in flames. Leona has one of the farms created on Douglas Station land and Fraser has a West Falkland farm. Jenny is in Stanley after many years at Johnson's Harbour not far from Tony's Estancia. June, too, is in Stanley and Jane has recently moved to the U.K. Finally, Tubby and Robin from Port Sussex have chosen Town but brother Sydney has opted for a sailor's life.

They and their children with all the others islanders are keeping the Falklands' future bright.

As Falkland Islanders, they have full internal self-government through their eight member Legislative Council, elected each four years. Their Development Corporation promotes the economy.

Fish have displaced sheep as the major source of income. Squid, happily feeding in the cold waters around the islands, are gobbled up by European and Far Eastern fishing boats. Beds of oysters and mussels are exploited for the shell-fish trade. Local fish is exported from a modern EU-approved processing plant.

A new abattoir in Stanley provides an outlet for mutton. A

hydroponic market garden supplies aubergines, tomatoes, peppers, cucumbers and lettuce to go with outdoor crops of potatoes, cabbage and cauliflowers where taste takes precedence over the shape, size and contour conformity required by so many of the world's supermarkets

Stanley has flourished; more houses and more facilities. The new school offers 16 subjects at GCSE level. From there, successful students can continue to college and university in Britain. The new hospital maintains a high standard with very modern facilities. Any patient needing specialist care in England is flown there for treatment.

For sport and fitness, there are the additions of a new swimming pool and gymnasium. The harbour provides for windsurfing, sailing and canoeing.

Nobody claims there are no imperfections in the islands or in the way of life. People are people wherever they live. Disregard for the common good can lead to misdemeanour or petty crime. In the Falklands, incidents are so rare they are almost non-existent.

Certainly justice in the islands can mete out a penalty suited to the offence. Crushing fines for driving over the limit, parents having to pay when their offspring cause thoughtless damage, prison for the criminal; an equable justice system making life better for everyone.

The islanders have forged forward. Like progressive people everywhere, they hail the improvements of modernity, saluting the new and perhaps barely noticing the passing ways of bygone days slipping quietly into memory.

At Britannia House, along Ross Road in Stanley, the museum of the Falkland Islands has its home. There, you can keep your place with the present and visit a time that is past.

Ah, yes. Peat smoke, subtle and comforting; tea-berries, cream and the sound of the waves sighing on the sand; bleating ewes calling for their lambs; a horse to ride; and the faithful wind.

Surely the wind is still there, the Falklands wind; and a people ever warm hearted and hospitable.

INDEX